MICHAEL BANNER

BRITAIN'S SLAVERY DEBT

reparations now!

OXFORD
UNIVERSITY PRESS

OXFORD
UNIVERSITY PRESS

Great Clarendon Street, Oxford, OX2 6DP,
United Kingdom

Oxford University Press is a department of the University of Oxford.
It furthers the University's objective of excellence in research, scholarship,
and education by publishing worldwide. Oxford is a registered trade mark of
Oxford University Press in the UK and in certain other countries

Published in the United States of America by Oxford University Press
198 Madison Avenue, New York, NY 10016, United States of America

British Library Cataloguing in Publication Data
Data available

Library of Congress Control Number: 2023945040

ISBN 978-0-19-888944-1

DOI: 10.1093/oso/9780198889441.001.0001

Printed and bound in the UK by
Clays Ltd, Elcograf S.p.A.

Links to third party websites are provided by Oxford in good faith and
for information only. Oxford disclaims any responsibility for the materials
contained in any third party website referenced in this work.

MIX
Paper | Supporting
responsible forestry
FSC
www.fsc.org   FSC® C018072

To the next generations:
Catherine, Lucy, Ciara, Orla, Ava, and Emilio
in the hope that their future will be more just than our past

FOREWORD

On 11 June 1833, at the conclusion of a very long and late sitting, the House of Commons voted to set aside £20,000,000 to be paid as compensation on the abolition of enslavement in the British colonies—chiefly in the Caribbean, the centre of the huge business of sugar.

One member of Parliament, Alexander Baring, expressed astonishment at the sum involved, but his intervention did not win a particularly sympathetic hearing. His confession that 'circumstances have not permitted me to be present at the debate this evening' was perhaps unfortunate, and produced what he termed a 'tumult'. He was undeterred however, and pressed on: 'Why, Sir', he exclaimed, 'the magnitude of the sum almost passes the powers of conception'—which, since he was himself a banker of some eminence and experience, was quite a claim. Given the present state of the country, he suggested, 'you might as well talk of £200,000,000'. This produced general laughter. The serious and seemingly now even more indignant Mr Baring insisted that 'voting away £20,000,000 is no laughing matter' and was 'surprised at the levity the House manifests upon the subject'. 'Honourable Members again laugh', he noted.[1]

The irony here is that Baring would be a beneficiary of compensation relating in particular to three plantations in St Kitts—he was questioning the enormity of a fund on which he would himself draw. For the compensation was to be paid not to those who had for the whole of their lives been deprived of any recompense for their labour, but to those who were set to lose their rights to the free labour of the enslaved which had made many of them very wealthy indeed.

It is the contention of this book that that £20,000,000 went to the wrong side. It was the enslaved, not the enslavers, who deserved compensation. But we are 200 years too late, someone might say. Well, yes, in certain respects—certainly too late for the generation of the enslaved who were uncompensated for the wrongs they suffered. But since that £20,000,000, like all the other wealth which enslavement generated, was mostly headed to Britain; and since, in addition, the heirs of those denied compensation were subsequently subjected to new forms of servitude and impoverishment; the money is still, two hundred years later, in the wrong place. It is my claim that focussing on that £20,000,000 provides us with a way of fixing on a sum which might just be the right starting place for negotiations on how to settle the still extant and unpaid debt.

This book, like the compensation owed to the enslaved, is very long overdue—but I don't mean by that what is usually meant when this is said in the foreword of a book. It normally means that the writer promised a manuscript to a publisher some time ago, and that delivery was somewhat behind schedule. In this case the manuscript was sent in on time. But it was late in a much more serious sense—what I am confessing is that it is only after forty years of academic life that I am now writing on topics which really deserved my attention a very long time ago.

My teaching and writing have been in the field of ethics, with a particular interest in the contribution of Christianity to moral thought and practice. I have written on all sorts of matters: on the ideas of particular thinkers such as Luther, Augustine, Karl Marx, and Friedrich Nietzsche, and on topics ranging from dementia to abortion, and from genetic modification to the ethics of death and dying. I have been concerned to reflect critically on such controversial practices as the use of animals in scientific experimentation, or the retention of human tissue after post mortem examination, and more general issues such as the proper valuation and protection of the environment, the having and not having of children, and the significance of mourning. In papers and chapters, in lectures and classes, I have discussed these questions and more, year in and year out. But never once, until less than two years ago, have I written or spoken on the subjects which concern this book, namely Britain's part in transatlantic enslavement and the racism which permitted and excused crimes against more than 12.5 million people.

My personal failing reflects a national failing. The period in which I was ignoring this issue was a period in which Britain itself manifestly failed to come to terms with its past. The bicentenary of the abolition of the slave trade in 2007 might have been a moment of reckoning. Historians had already begun to chart the horrors of the slave trade and the harsh regime of exploitation of enslaved labour on plantations which that trade supplied. And yet still the bicentenary was an occasion for 'self-congratulation' which 'effectively displaced a sense of national responsibility for Britain's involvement in colonial slavery'.[2] Black writers and activists who tried to open a conversation about reparations, were mostly ignored. To put it more starkly, Britain preferred to celebrate certain happy bits of its history rather than to notice the suffering, injustice, and exploitation which this history had also involved.

It is hard to see this failure to face up to the past as other than an expression of the racism which was central to the practice of slavery itself. In the forty years prior to 2007, in the early part of which I was growing up, what is sometimes referred to as 'casual racism' was very much the norm. It seems better to me to speak of 'everyday racism'. A casual affair is one in which the parties may go their separate ways at any time; a casual worker is one who works as and when, but is not a permanent employee; a casual remark is one which is not very considered or not to be taken seriously. The racism with which I grew up was not casual in these senses, for it was neither occasional, marginal, nor lightly held. And this everyday racism was ubiquitous, and it was very effectively propagated not through some explicit catechism or official teaching, but as voiced in everyday observations, judgements, and assumptions.

Anti-semitic remarks were a commonplace, repeating well-known (and medieval, if not earlier) tropes about money, wealth, and business dealings; a racial slur might be used to refer to the colour of a carpet or sofa (as D.H. Lawrence used it in *England, My England* in 1922 to identify the colour of a dress) or, referring to a person in a wood pile, would indicate a tricky problem; jungles would be identified as the original and rightful home of certain groups of people; Romanies (called gypsies) would be referred to in derogatory terms; Enoch Powell may have been sacked from the front bench of the Conservative party (in 1968) for his infamous 'rivers of blood' speech, and for his advocacy of repatriation, but he was the most popular politician of his day and was spoken of not as a pariah but as a voice in the wilderness, raising for debate matters which no one else had the courage to address; and the plights of Rhodesia (as it then was) and South Africa were definitely not the plights of their majorities but of their minorities in staving off majority rule. These conversational commonplaces might be heard in homes, classrooms, shops, or workplaces—and I don't remember them being challenged, certainly not routinely. Predictably the language of the playground was even more crude and stark—an Iranian contemporary of mine, who attended what certain newspapers would doubtless refer to as one of our 'leading public schools', tells me he was routinely addressed by means of the abbreviation of the name for a soft doll popular in the nineteenth century, with a dark face, gaudy dress, and abundant hair (an image of which still adorned jars of marmalade until 2001), and that he generally failed to discombobulate his taunters even when he pointed out that his ancestors had been living in spectacular cities at a time when theirs had aspired to mud huts.

Why does a particular academic pursue one question and not another? Why does a nation remember some aspects of its history and ignore others? What we notice and fail to notice, what we take seriously and what we overlook—these are matters the explanation of which may require some subtlety. But it seems at least plausible to connect the disregard of something as significant as the forcible transportation of 12.5 million people to enforced labour and early deaths on the other side of the Atlantic as the continuing legacy of the racism which was embedded in the practice of slavery itself. If as individuals and as a nation we chose to look the other way, it was perhaps because we had consciously or unconsciously absorbed the idea which the diehard defenders of enslavement had maintained back in the day, that enslavement really wasn't a grave wrong at all.

Personally and nationally, reckoning with the horrors of enslavement is long overdue—and reckoning with the horrors of enslavement, so this book contends, also means reckoning, nearly two hundred years after the event, with the failure of Parliament's package of compensation to end up in the right hands. It is the burden of my argument that the wrongdoing in which Britain played a key and even leading role as a colonial power is not in fact just a bit of our long-gone history. Rather this history lives on in the harms still borne by the descendants of the enslaved, and in the benefits still enjoyed by modern-day Britons. Those to whom compensation was properly due nearly two hundred years ago received nothing and the money ended up in the wrong hands. It is time to put that right.

ACKNOWLEDGEMENTS

An invitation to give a paper to the Society for the Study of Christian Ethics in late 2021 first encouraged me to turn to the themes of this book. The conference theme was truth, and I am not at all sure what I intended when I agreed to give a paper, but by the time it was due, an interest in the notion of doing the truth directed me towards the issue of reparations. I am grateful to the participants at that session for their critical engagement with my paper and to Brian Brock of the University of Aberdeen for written comments.

Robert Song prodded me to take things further by inviting me to present to a seminar in the University of Durham. Sabine Cadeau (now of McGill University) asked me to give a paper under the auspices of University of Cambridge's Legacies of Enslavement project, and has been a generous guide to many of the issues on which she is an expert authority. Henning Grosse Ruse-Khan, of King's College, Cambridge, was a learned and helpful respondent to that paper. My initial findings about Trinity College's entanglements with enslavement were presented to the immensely valuable conference which marked the conclusion of the first stage of the University of Cambridge's enquiries and again I am grateful to Sabine Cadeau for the invitation to participate. I am also grateful to Professor Cadeau for generously sharing her findings regarding Isaac Newton and Robert Smith as part of her wider findings as the chief researcher on the University's project; I also acknowledge with thanks the insights and information shared with me by Dr Nicolas Bell-Romero, Sabine Cadeau's co-researcher. I gave a similar paper to meetings in New York and Tokyo and benefitted from lively debate.

My colleagues at Trinity College had seemed variously perplexed, troubled, or hostile to my interest in the College's hitherto uncovered connections with enslavement until I presented those same initial findings to an open meeting of the Fellowship, with academics across the range of disciplines. That meeting produced critical and constructive discussion and commentary, and enabled me to sharpen my thoughts on many issues, and I hope to publish a book in the near future telling the story of Trinity, enslavement, and its legacies. Meanwhile I am grateful to the Master and Fellows for a period of sabbatical leave which allowed me to complete this book, and for the College's general and generous support of all aspects of research. Amongst my colleagues at Trinity I am especially grateful to Joshua Heath and Rupert Gatti for discussions of various topics, to Louise Merrett for her careful and insightful reading of a draft, and to John Lonsdale for sharing something of his vast knowledge of the history of Africa. Anthea Smith read and commented on the final draft with her usual eagle-eyed attention to detail. Joel Robbins is an unfailing source of encouragement and wisdom.

I received thoughtful and reflective comments on a draft from G.J. Barker Benfield of the State University of New York and Ike Achebe of Hunter College, City University of New York. J.C. de Swaan of Princeton provided gentle and considerate guidance over a number of conversations. Two Cambridge research students, Leroy Levy and Akeem Adagbada, engaged critically and

constructively with the issues of the book, as did two of my distinguished senior colleagues, Esra Ozyurek and David Fergusson.

Oxford University Press's reader rightly encouraged me to
stress that, as I mention in the foreword, I (with most of those who
would be racialized as 'white'), am late to this issue, whereas
writers and activists from the African diaspora have been speaking
and campaigning on reparations for very many years. I acknowledge this point through comments and references throughout
the book, but it is good to say up front and in clear terms that this
work is merely an attempt to provide support to those who have
laboured in the field and provided moral leadership long before
I took this question seriously.

Sally-Ann Gannon didn't really need to read a draft, and has no
need to read the book, since she has much more than merely tol-
erantly lived with its concerns and arguments day by day, week by
week, and month by month. The contrast between the regular
and, I fear, sometimes taken for granted, joys of family life, and the
abusive disregard of community and kinship about which I have
been writing, has felt at times extreme and painful. It surely
should, and indeed does, sharpen one's appreciation of those joys,
shared with Sally and with the next generations, to whom this
book is lovingly dedicated.

CONTENTS

The Caribbean call for reparations will resonate with increasing intensity in the political and diplomatic corridors of British-Caribbean relations until it is answered and matters brought to a settlement by means of formal resolution. The evidentiary basis of the case has long been established. It points overwhelmingly to the conclusion that Britain and other colonizing and slave-owning European nations have a case to answer in respect of the multiple crimes against humanity they committed in the region.

Hilary Beckles, *How Britain Underdeveloped the Caribbean*

1

Introduction

A Proposal

This book contends that Britain owes reparations to the Caribbean. Slavery was also practised by, and compensation was paid to, planters in Mauritius, the Cape of Good Hope, Bermuda, and the Bahamas, but these places have particular histories raising particular issues, and I shall focus on the Caribbean to which just about 83% of the claims for compensation related.

The broad case for Britain making such reparation is relatively simple and involves an historical and a moral claim. The historical claim is that the exploitation of generations of the islands' inhabitants under slavery and colonialism wronged those people while enriching Britain—and crucially, that as we are the inheritors of these riches, so present generations in the Caribbean are inheritors of relative poverty.

It was enslaved Africans who provided labour for the brutal but immensely profitable sugar plantations. The wealth to be made from these plantations ensured that these small and distant islands became the treasured possessions of Europe's colonial powers—and, to use Gary Nash's resonant phrase, turned 'a Caribbean Garden of Eden' into a 'living hell'.[1] The passage of the 1833 Abolition of Slavery Act was indeed a significant moment in the history of the Caribbean and of the British empire; but whereas former purported owners of slaves received vast sums in compensation (money that would fund the second wave of the British industrial revolution), the enslaved received nothing. Furthermore, they were, even after abolition, effectively bound into a form of tied labour which would oppress them in the same way that emancipated African Americans were oppressed in the Confederate States after the failure of reconstruction. Even in the last period of empire, Britain sought to maintain a relationship with the Caribbean based on its understanding of colonies as producers of raw materials and consumers of manufactured goods from the motherland: development was not a significant goal of colonial policy. In other words, the relationship between Britain and the Caribbean, from beginning to end, was governed throughout by what Beckles terms 'extractive colonialism'—the legacy of which is 'persistent poverty'.[2]

Racism was, of course, the enabling doctrine that subtended this story and is part of the history that Britain has failed to confront. It is this failure to acknowledge, let alone to come to terms with, this history, which, in my experience, underlies initial and somewhat knee-jerk resistance to the case for reparations. To feel the force of the case, Britons would have to know just how bad it really was.

The moral claim—the point of principle if you like—is that where a moral wrong or harm has been done or committed, an act of moral repair is called for. In crude terms, and in an everyday context which we all understand, moral repair means saying sorry with a bunch of flowers in your hand—we just know that this, or some similar gesture, is the right thing to do if we forgot to show up for a lunch we arranged some time ago with a friend. In the case of graver wrongs, and in a more formal context, what is demanded is 'restitution' or 'reparation'—and the notion of reparations is a familiar one in thinking about the restoration of relationships not between individuals or neighbours, but between nations. Britain harmed the people of the Caribbean over a long period, and even now we are the continuing beneficiaries of that harm—just as the current inhabitants of the region continue to suffer as a result of this history. Moral repair is owed, and reparations are due.

If this is the simple case for reparations (to be made in Chapters 2 and 3), my experience in making this simple case is that it encounters a regular set of objections. Some of the objections are to the very notion of making or paying of reparations; others address the practicality (or supposed impracticality) of doing so. Both sets of objections need answering if the case is to succeed.

The objections in principle to making reparations are mostly very familiar: 'it's a long time ago—time to move on'; 'slavery was legal back then, so there can be no question of making amends for it now'; 'we weren't the worst slavers or colonialists'; 'what about the Vikings?—how will we get them to pay up?'; 'rather than banging on about reparations, shouldn't we be celebrating Britain's leading role in the abolition of the slave trade and slavery?'—and so on. Though these objections are not, in fact, very weighty, it is important to answer them one by one, since they seem to have a certain currency—certainly they recur again and again whenever the case for reparations is put.

Requiring longer consideration are three rather more weighty objections to reparations. First, there is the thought that reparations are objectionable, at least in the case of very grave harms, as simply incommensurable with the harm done, and therefore as not just inappropriate but sometimes downright offensive.

3

(This thought played a key role in the case against Israel accepting reparations from the Germans after WWII.) Second, it is often said that intergenerational reparations are wrong as 'visiting the sins of the fathers on the children'. These two objections deserve more extended discussion so as to clarify issues of responsibility, guilt and shame, as well as to acknowledge the limits of moral repair. In the third place there is a more subtle objection which needs to be faced, which says that reparations across racial lines risk perpetuating the very racial divide which has led to reparations being demanded in the first place—this claim may connect up with the thought that reparations are altogether simply back-ward looking, when we had better look forward and focus on righting existing, not historic, wrongs. Addressing this collection of doubts about reparations is the work for Chapter 4.

I have found in discussion that many who understand and acknowledge the historical claim, and accept the case for repar-ations in principle, nonetheless find practical questions more vexed. *Who* should pay *what* to *whom*? As often happens, what may be thought a good idea at first sight, sinks under the weight of practical concerns as to how it is going to work in reality. It is vital then, to take up the challenge of addressing these practical diffi-culties in Chapter 5 and to focus in turn on who should do the paying, on what should be paid, and to whom.

Reparations are not only, or not even, of course, always, about money. And in the case of the Caribbean, CARICOM (the body charged by a confederation of Caribbean nations with pressing the case for reparations), proposes a much wider suite of meas-ures and initiatives than mere payments as beginning to right the wrongs of the past. Yet money is part of it, and it is often over money that the argument seems to founder—what sum is plausible, appropriate, or affordable? A good starting point, I will suggest, is provided by the sum of £20 million which the British government set aside in 1834 as compensation not to those who had been enslaved, but as compensation to their purported owners for the loss of their labour. £20 million was a huge sum—the Bank of England's inflation calculator reckons it as £1.9 billion in modern day values, though if that sum were compounded at 4%, as if it had been soundly invested, the original sum would today be worth closer to £30 billion. Of course, the compensation paid to the owners was only for loss of labour. The enslaved lost not only the value of their labour, but much else besides, suffering the traumas of dislocation, violence, and bondage. Moreover, that £20 million relates to only one generation of enslaved people—those 650,000 or thereabouts, alive at the moment of emancipation. In total Britain transported more than 2.3 million Africans to the Caribbean, and many more to North and South America—and even after emancipation, ways were found to bind those formerly enslaved into exploitative patterns of employment amounting to new forms of servitude. Nonetheless I contend that, working with £20 million as a starting point, it is possible to arrive at a sum or range of sums for material reparations. Any such sum is inevitably no more than a token—and money could only ever be one element in what reparations should be. But taking that £20m seriously and working with it provides a basis for arriving at a provisional figure to begin serious discussions between Britain and the Caribbean.

Finally, in Chapter 6, the book will address the 'healthy realism' or cynicism (whichever way you look at it), which brushes the whole matter of reparations aside with the thought 'it ain't gonna happen'. The realist—or cynic—will surely be impatient with the arguments so far advanced and will likely contend that, in the much invoked 'real world', no one will step up or pay up. Indeed the USA and Britain, for example, have both been quite explicit in saying that reparations are not the way to address any grievances which other nations may have against them.

The irony is, of course, that the realist of the 1770s scoffed at the notion that slavery and the slave trade could or would be abolished. The transatlantic trade in enslaved people was, as the early campaigners gathered to plot against it, at the very height of its commercial success and economic significance. And yet, though it was long in coming, abolition occurred within the lifetime of some of the early campaigners.

This chapter makes the point, then, that realism is, in fact, often unrealistic. The campaign for reparations is perhaps in its early stages. Yet there are things that can and should be done, here and now, in particular by institutions below the level of national governments, to advance the case for reparations between governments. Such steps would themselves begin to address the wrongs of the past, and model to the UK government what a national programme of reparations would look like. There is no guarantee that any campaign will succeed in ensuring that the nation faces up to its responsibilities for the past and its enduring legacies—no more could those campaigners of 250 years ago be certain of achieving their objectives. And yet they were finally successful, and what was dismissed as pie in the sky utopianism became national policy.

* * *

The considerable fortune of the conservative Member of Parliament for South Dorset, Richard Drax, has its origins in the huge wealth amassed by one of the pioneers in the sugar trade, Sir James Drax. The energetic founder of the family fortune acquired substantial estates in Barbados, purchased enslaved people in 1642, and by the 1650s had established on his Drax Hall estate a way of deploying enslaved peoples which would spread across the Caribbean as sugar became the most valuable crop in the trade between the colonies and Europe. Sugar plantations would come to net huge profits for their owners, while consuming the lives of enslaved people in one of the most brutal and relentless slave regimes found anywhere in the world. At the end of the eighteenth century slave owners resisted the abolition of the slave trade, and then emancipation—but when emancipation came, they drove a hard bargain and received (the recipients including another of Richard Drax's forebears), considerable cash down in recompense for the loss of their 'chattels', as they would have put it.

Nearly 400 years after the original crime, and nearly 200 years after emancipation, it has been suggested that the current beneficiary of the inheritance should give up the house and estate from which it all started. But when he is asked about his inheritance, the MP tends to fob off the issue: 'I am keenly aware of the slave trade in the West Indies, and the role my very distant ancestor played in it is deeply, deeply regrettable, but no one can be held responsible today for what happened many hundreds of years ago. This is a part of the nation's history, from which we must all learn.'[3]

The ironies in this posture are multiple—the most outstanding being perhaps, that Mr Drax's claim to his 400-year-old inheritance relies on a respect for the sanctity of property and family which it was of the very of essence of chattel slavery to deny. The right of an enslaved man or woman to property in their labour was disregarded under enslavement, and the bonds of family were routinely desecrated. In claiming the right to hold on to his ill-gotten gains, Mr Drax appeals to sentiments and notions that the enterprise of enslavement systematically denied and flouted.

More to the point immediately, however, is the sad fact that in woefully evading the issue, Mr Drax is only doing as an individual what has been done by all the countries who had a part in the slave trade. At the bicentenary of its abolition in 2007, Tony Blair expressed his 'deep sorrow' for Britain's role, describing it as 'profoundly shameful'.[4] But he failed to signal any proper reckoning with Britain's more than 250 years at the forefront of Atlantic trade in enslaved people. The bicentenary—engaging in what Ta-Nehisi Coates terms 'à la carte patriotism'[5]—was designed solely to celebrate the achievement of Wilberforce, Clarkson, et al., in bringing an end to the horrors of slavery, while neatly overlooking the fact that Britons were amongst the leading perpetrators of those horrors. With this rather important fact left on the side lines, the question of making recompense for those horrors can be more easily ignored than faced.

Of course, many other European nations had a part in the long and profitable slave trade; and yet no European nation has yet seriously entertained, let alone conceded, the case for reparations. And yet that case, I will suggest, not only deserves a hearing but is compelling.

There are three important caveats to the argument that follows, one word to be said about language, and a reflection on the calculations and numbers which provide something of the substance of the demand for reparations.

First, it should be obvious already that making the case for reparations, and answering objections to it, involves straying over a huge territory. It requires, at the very least, engagement with

ethics and history, as well as touching on questions which belong
to the spheres of economics, political theory and practice, juris-
prudence, social policy, and more. No one person making the case
for reparations can do so without taking the risks involved in leaving one's home turf—and I, as an ethicist with a particular interest
in religion and social anthropology, inevitably do just that in making the case from beginning to end. But there is great merit, I
believe, in trying to make the case as a whole in one fell swoop. I
have found in discussion that sceptics as to the merits of reparations, answered on one point or another in argument, quickly
relocate the really crucial difficulties as lying in another place.
There is merit, then, in all the parts of the case being presented
together, just to discourage any such evasions—but let me admit
at the outset the risk, albeit one worth taking, of arguing beyond
the reach of one's limited competencies.

Second, it follows, given the many and various elements that
make up the argument, that to do anything like justice to the case,
a very long book indeed would be necessary. The required tome
might run to many hundreds of pages and be laden down with
learned footnotes. Such a work would have its worth. But the present state of the argument suggests that there is reason for offering
a short book such as this one, which attempts to make the case
concisely and clearly. Once the case for reparations is widely
agreed to be plausible, detailed consideration of especially the
practical aspects of recompense will become urgent. But until that
general case is presented compellingly in short order, and accepted
as prima facie plausible, such a comprehensive analysis seems pre-
mature.

There is a quite different and third point which also needs to be
acknowledged and underlined. The case for reparations is not new

even if it has not yet won general acceptance—and it has been made clearly and powerfully, especially by those who suffered as a result of the practices of enslavement and colonialism, including the descendants of the enslaved.[6] Someone such as myself, who would be racialized as 'white' in our common racist schema, contributes to the discussion not with a view to correcting those who have pioneered the way, but rather as having learnt from them, and in (belated) solidarity with a movement which has a long and powerful history. But arguments, even while they draw on pre-existing discussions, are always specific to an individual and their context—and the following case for reparations is an intervention made from my particular place and to my particular time. It has benefitted from a considerable body of existing work advanced by many others, and does not pretend to be wholly novel or original, even if it hopes to be fresh and brisk. Its most important claim is that the case for reparations can be set out in simple form, that it is strong in principle and as a practical proposition, and indeed compelling—so that the time for reparations is now.

As to language: it is very difficult to talk about the history of all this without using language which can seem to deny or efface the horrors, for such the traditional language certainly did. The word 'slave' may seem to name a class of being rather than someone on whom a wrong has been perpetrated, so there is now a general preference for speaking of an 'enslaved person'. As I shall say later in the book, the word 'plantation' to describe the site of the exploitation and abuse of the enslaved, risks concealing the reality of that exploitation behind a rather neutral term. In another way, referring to 'slave owners' seems to concede their ownership—my preference would be to talk of 'purported owners of enslaved people', to register the presumptions involved. For all that, these linguistic cautions are in danger of creating cumbersome and clunky sentences, so I have sometimes, for the sake of brevity, used older terms and shorthand, without for a minute admitting the moral presumptions which they may be said to contain, nor wishing to conceal the horrors they have served to hide.

Last of all, before we turn to the case in more detail, there is a terrible irony to be admitted straight up. And that is that the calculations which I engage in to generate what might be deemed a suitable sum for reparations, echo—albeit in a different key—the calculations which were at the heart of the business of trafficking in people and enslaving them. Slave traders saw the enslaved as cargo. Plantation owners listed the enslaved alongside other 'stock'. Returning a profit on the cargo and the stock was the central calculation. Human beings had become items on a balance sheet.

In the search for a recompense for the continuing harms of this history, I find myself venturing calculations relating to human lives marred, blighted and lost. Such calculations, echoing the original computations, ought to be unsettling—but for the sake of trying to right a wrong, and conscious of the seeming repetition of enslavement's misrepresentation of human worth, on to this tricky ground we must tread.

2

Britain and the Caribbean

A Brief (and Painful) History

Britain and the Caribbean: A Story in Three Acts

The story of Britain and the Caribbean is a history in three acts—but the stage for this history was set by the immediately preceding colonial adventure spearheaded by the Spanish.

Columbus's arrival in what he took to be the Indies in 1492, whatever his intentions, caused a radical rupture in the life of peoples and cultures which had flourished for more than 800 years before this encounter. Modern scholars term these inhabitants of the Caribbean the Taíno. They were displaced, decimated by disease, and pressed into hard labour in mines and on farms in service of colonial interests. The enslavement of the indigenous people was a matter of moral controversy in Spain. Not so the enslavement of the West Africans who were brought to the Caribbean as early as 1500, and who increasingly provided the labour to replace that of the declining indigenous populations—who were, in any case, judged variously resistant, recalcitrant, or unreliable as workers.

Britain played no significant part in this period. The Spanish and Portuguese were the first movers in the Atlantic trade in enslaved people, and it was the Spanish whose failed colonization of the Caribbean contributed to the virtual erasure of the existing peoples and culture—though the British and others would take up where the Spanish had left off. Whoever played what part, 'by the beginning of the seventeenth century', says Higman, 'European colonization had reduced the Caribbean islands to a blank canvas.... The land that had been brought to a high state of cultivation by the Taínos was being reconquered by rainforest.'[1]

Act I: Slavery and Sugar

From the British perspective, the story of the Caribbean begins with that relatively blank canvas and the waning of Spanish power. It was this dual opening which allowed Britain and other would-be colonial powers to gain first a toe hold on the lesser islands, which were practically beneath the regard of the older great powers, and to initiate there what has been termed the 'sugar revolution'—the developments in agriculture, trade, and the use of enslaved labour, which, in succession and in contrast to the failed colonialism of the earlier period, turned the Caribbean into a source of immense wealth for the new colonial powers.

With the founding of a colony in Barbados in 1625 and in the acquisition of Jamaica in 1655, Britain was at the forefront of developing systems of plantation management for labour-hungry sugar, perfecting the exploitation of enslaved labour from West Africa in a brutal regime of production and processing. To begin with the enslaved labourers were typically bought from and shipped by other nations. But if Britain had not been there at the beginning of that trade in human bodies, it was quick to catch up. By the mid seventeenth century and for nearly two hundred years thereafter, Britain had a leading place in the trafficking of Africans to supply its own, and other nations', booming plantations.

Supply and use were two sides of this sordid business.

On the supply side, Britain, though relatively late to the game, eventually became the key player in trafficking enslaved people for much of the century preceding the trade's abolition within the British empire in 1807. English adventurers—such as Sir John Hawkins—had led slave-raiding expeditions on the west coast of Africa back in the 1560s, and in the early 1600s various companies were established and given royal charters to pursue the so-called 'Guinea' trade. The successors to these companies at the end of the seventeenth and early eighteenth centuries built on these beginnings, and the South Sea Company, engaging in the trade in the period 1714 to 1739, shipped upwards of 34,000 people. Alongside these officially supported ventures, private traders, operating chiefly out of London, then Bristol, and then Liverpool, came to dominate the growing business—and prior to the abolition of the slave trade, Liverpool was the world's major slaving port. In the peak years, something like 43,500 enslaved people were transported annually on British ships.[2] Over a period of more than four hundred years around 12.5 million Africans were carried across the Atlantic—and perhaps 25% of this 'merchandise', as the British merchants would have termed it, in British ships.

It was a commonplace, even in the ancient world which was generally uncritical of enslavement, to look with disdain on slave traders, and so in the eighteenth century. Slave-trading was manifestly a rough and violent affair. The British traders rarely ventured far from their ships, and the enslaved people they bought from local suppliers had been gathered sometimes from considerable distances. They had been captured in war or simply kidnapped;

others were enslaved as punishment or to settle debts. Many of these captives died before they reached the coast to be shipped; many died on the notorious Middle Passage which brought them to the Americas—as many as 25% in the early years, falling to 10% as an average in the eighteenth century.[3] The voyage, lasting typically somewhere between four to six weeks, was one of horror for those chained in dark squalor below the decks, and terror for those above. The ship's crew might themselves succumb to the diseases which ravaged those they were transporting, but they also feared the resistance which the enslaved often mounted against their capture and incarceration. The guns on slave ships pointed on to the decks, not out to sea.

Those who survived the voyage might then be sold on a quay-side, destined to they knew not where or what. If—against the odds—they had maintained ties of family, friendship, or ethnicity thus far, those bonds would now quite likely be sundered. Slave owners showed no respect for family connections (while highly conscious of nurturing their own) and positively sought to break up ethnic affiliation, since differences of language in their work gangs were thought to inhibit the conversion of grievances into coordinated rebellion.

Such were the well-known horrors of the Middle Passage which inspired the first abolitionist campaign. Early efforts aimed at the amelioration of the conditions on slaving ships—thus Sir William Dolben's private member's bill of 1788 sought to regulate the number of enslaved people to be packed on board slaving vessels and to provide for the presence of a surgeon on such voyages. The measure just made it on to the statute book—it had been opposed by the so-called West Indian Interest and subject to numerous amendments in the House of Lords. But the trade continued in

barely mitigated brutality till its so-called abolition in 1807—
although the abolition was, in fact, only of the transatlantic trade
in human bodies. Scholars estimate that 20,000 enslaved people
were traded between the islands in the next twenty-five years leading up to the second abolition, of slavery itself, and trading within
a colony continued as before.[4]

If the supply side of the business was grim, the use made of
those who got to the other side (as we might aptly term it), only
continued the horror. Early English colonialism had relied on
indentured servants from Britain—typically young people who
agreed to serve for a period of years perhaps in the hope of establishing themselves on their own account at the end of their service. But sugar was a demanding crop and plantation owners
quickly turned to enslaved workers as more reliably meeting their
needs. Indentured labourers were more expensive than slaves
(they only served for a fixed term) and as populations declined
after the English Civil War, surplus workers were harder to find or
to tempt to the colonies and especially to the work of the sugar
plantations.

The work of these plantations was gruelling, the conditions
were harsh, and lives of the enslaved were typically bitter and
short.

From planting to cropping, sugar production demanded heavy
and intensive labour. Clearing the ground and establishing the
new crop was work for the very strongest, but it was the harvesting, perhaps fourteen months later, which made the greatest calls
on the workforce. Sugar canes deteriorate very quickly after cut-
ting, so the heavy labour of harvesting in the daytime would be
followed by nighttime work in the factories which crushed the
stalks, boiled the juice, and produced raw sugar. Some of the work

required considerable knowledge and aptitude, and some was dangerous—hot sugar burns and rollers crush not only stalks of cane. All of the work was exhausting—and eventually, for most of the workforce, debilitating.

It is well known that as many as one-third of newly imported workers died in their first year or eighteen months in the colonies during what was termed their 'seasoning'. What also needs noting is that early deaths were the norm for the entire workforce. Slaveholders would regularly resist any regulation of plantations and working conditions by insisting that owners of chattels could be relied upon to look after their own property. Even abolitionists were tempted by this seeming piece of common sense. In fact, however, the economics of slave-owning meant that plantation owners found it more efficient and effective to purchase newly enslaved workers from traders than to sustain the existing population and renew them through breeding. It is striking that, whereas slave populations in the mainland colonies in America were early on sustained by natural growth, the Caribbean populations were not. Malnutrition, disease, overwork, and high infant mortality all played a part. Thus, 'by 1790 Barbados, Jamaica, and the Leewards had taken a total of some 1,230,000 slaves from Africa in order to achieve a collective black population of about 387,000'.[5]

The mention of high infant mortality makes passing reference, in effect, to the particular burden which fell on women among the enslaved. At any stage from capture to sale in the Caribbean, women might be separated from existing offspring. Once on the plantation they could resist the coercive sexual attentions of owners and overseers only at the risk of the everyday violence, which, as I shall mention presently, was meted out as a matter of course.[6] Little or no allowance was made for pregnant women, either in expectations of work or in the punishments they might receive—though some plantations dug holes in the ground to accommodate pregnant women who were to be whipped, this being a concession since the usual practice was to hang the victim of punishment with toes barely touching the ground.[7] And a woman's ability to care for a child, however conceived, or even to keep it, was also wholly subject to the will or whim of owners.[8]

Campaigners had always believed that abolition of the slave trade would improve the lot of slaves—slave owners would surely take care of chattels which were no longer so easy to replace. It was that same common sense again. 'The reality', writes Gad Heuman, 'was very different'. Even after the abolition of the trade in human bodies, 'British West Indian colonies, apart from Barbados and the Bahamas, failed to maintain a positive natural increase in the slave population in the period 1816 to 1834. While there were some significant variations from colony to colony, the heaviest decreases occurred in those areas dominated by sugar plantations.'[9] Low birth rates and high mortality continued to be the norm.

The regime of ceaseless toil under harsh conditions was maintained, as slave-owners knew it only ever could be, by the ever-present whip, and by threats of punishment which were brutal even by the standards of the time. Higman's account is graphic but necessary:

> On the plantations...whipping was common, the lash wielded by the hand of the driver. Aggravated atrocities such as the rubbing of salt, lime and pepper into open wounds were regularly practiced. Being shackled or chained to heavy iron weights made escape physically impossible or at least excruciatingly painful. Being

placed in bilboes or stocks was even more immobilizing. Individual slave owners and their employees were often barbaric in their treatment of enslaved people, adding excruciating pain to social indignity. The most severe whippings resulted in death or physical disability. Some were forced to swallow piss and shit, others had limbs or genitals chopped off, or were buried alive up to the neck. The desire to instil fear in order to extract the maximum amount of labour and profit slid easily into unrestrained brutality and sadism.[10]

Such was what we might term the day-to-day violence of the plantation, but more exceptional circumstances and times produced even more extremes of cruelty. Any enslaved person who was not cowed, or killed, by routine punishments might be sold off to another island or even into enslavement in a Spanish colony on the South American mainland. This second separation from kith and kin was understood to be a hard burden, and, like all the punishments, aimed as much at deterring others as at any other end. Open revolt, or at least suspicion of it, produced pitiless retribution marked by almost limitless barbarity and viciousness. Burning to death was a favoured means of punishment, extended as long as possible to make the most of the spectacle. As far as one can tell, the only limits placed on such punishments were the limits of unrestrained and brutal imaginations.

The slave trade supplied what we term the plantations, but that rather coy word 'plantation' conceals the fact that the horrors of the notorious Middle Passage were just a prelude to horrors quite as shocking as those of the voyage. It would be more telling to refer to the plantations as slave labour prison camps, to avoid any picturesque connotations which the word 'plantation' may convey. And yet even that unwieldy wording fails to convey the full character of the regimes which prevailed for much of the period.

Once we note the plantation-owners preference for taking new shipments of Africans over maintaining those they already had—the fact, as Higman puts it, that 'the Caribbean sugar plantation colonies gobbled up enslaved people, and were never satisfied'[11]—then we find ourselves reaching after an even more cumbersome but satisfactorily descriptive neologism. The plantations were slave labour prison death camps.

The irony in all this story, of course, is that the bitter suffering of those who were carried to and worked the Caribbean's fields supplied European tables with the sweetness of sugar. Once, sugar had been a rare luxury item. But as the seventeenth and eighteenth centuries progressed, the sugar revolution met a more general demand to render palatable the harsh taste of two other colonial products, coffee and tea, and finally reached even the tables of the poor, especially in England—for whom sweetened tea and bread and jam would become staples.

The trade was immense—and immensely profitable. By 1700 the British islands of Barbados, Jamaica, Antigua, Nevis, and Monserrat were producing close to half of the world's sugar exports—by 1770, Caribbean exports of sugar had increased absolutely and as a share of total global output. By the middle of the century, sugar was the most valuable commodity in European trade—and although increased production to meet ever rising demand led to falls in prices, sugar production yielded vast fortunes over nearly two centuries, both to individuals and to nations.

Individually, those colonizers who survived the challenges of climate, disease, and excessive consumption of alcohol, did well—the average white Jamaican in 1774 was worth more than £1000; back home his compatriot was worth only £42.[12] And these successful West Indians were famous for their opulence and conspicuous consumption—Fonthill Abbey in Wiltshire, the seat of an absentee heir of great estates in Jamaica (William Thomas Beckford, described by the newspapers as the 'richest commoner in England'), was perhaps the epitome of excess and folly. (The building's extraordinary central tower was built and rebuilt twice before collapsing a third time—though Beckford, by now in debt, had been forced to sell before the final ruination.) But Beckford's epic achievement in conspicuous consumption was echoed, and only slightly more modestly, by countless others in the 200 years of enslavement in the West Indies. In the islands themselves the leading plantation owners impressed each other and visitors with their grand residences, their vast personal retinues of enslaved servants, and the excess of their entertainments, supplied as they were with the very finest food and the choicest of wines. But the planters were very often, as it has been said, 'reluctant creoles'[13]— that is, they never really settled to the idea of permanent residence in the islands, even if they were Caribbean born. They typically wanted to head 'home', even if for a first visit. And on establishing themselves in Britain, the West Indians maintained their reputation for lavish lifestyles and seemingly limitless funds. Harewood House in Yorkshire, still in the possession of the Lascelles family, is just one of many stately homes which converted wealth from the grubby world of slave-trading plantations into the respectable solidity of an English country seat of considerable grandeur.

The measure to which the sugar islands contributed to the wealth of the nation is a more contested matter. The immediate contribution of sugar to the national coffers was by way of the duty paid by producers and importers. But there was a much wider contribution to the economy as a whole. If sugar was the centre of the whole business, its production relied on a host of other products, provisions, and services. Manufactured items from across Britain, ranging from iron goods to small arms to cloth, were the currency used in West Africa in the trade for kidnapped people. The ships which carried the goods to West Africa and the new cargo to the West Indies were built, provisioned, and manned from British ports. The plantations themselves needed clothes and food for their labourers, and timber, building materials, and all the equipment for their sugar works—as well as the luxury goods to satisfy the demands of the successful planters. Ironware came from the Midlands, beef came from Ireland, salted fish from British fisheries, and clothes from Lancashire and Scotland. And all of this hectic to and fro of trade relied on banking services and insurance to oil the wheels.

Some (most famously Eric Williams in his seminal contribution) have seen the monies flowing from the plantations as fuelling the industrial revolution.[14] Others have thought that the main drivers of British economic expansion were independent of these nonetheless highly prized islands. A long debate has gone in one direction or the other over nearly eighty years. Morgan provides a balanced assessment when he notes that 'Caribbean-based demand may have accounted for about 35 per cent of the growth of total British exports between 1748 and 1776, and for about 12 per cent of the increase in British industrial output in the quarter-century before the American Revolution.... [T]he slave-sugar trading complex strengthened the British economy and played a significant, though not decisive part, in its evolution.' More recently Klas Rönnbäck has estimated that economic activities directly associated with the triangular trade (namely 'the exports of manufactures to Africa, the trade in slaves across the Atlantic, and the exports of raw materials to Europe', and thus including the activity on the American mainland), added some 11% to British GDP during the first decade of the nineteenth century.[15]

To whatever degree, no part of the British economy was untouched by a business which spanned and connected a global empire and trading network. And one thing is very clear. The planters and their backers in Westminster opposed the abolition of the trade in enslaved people, and then the abolition of enslavement itself, on the grounds that the well-being of the plantations was a matter not only of private, but of national, interest. Sugar may once have been a luxury reserved for the very wealthy, but in virtue of the sugar revolution it had come to seem a necessary and commonplace item in most diets even though it contributed nothing of nutritional value—and the duties paid on it had come to seem a regular and vital source of government revenue. The cost of the callous trade to those who were transported across the Atlantic and subjected to the brutal regime of the plantations was quite extraordinary. But it was a cost which, prior to abolition, the slaving nations of western Europe were willing to bear—or rather, were willing for others to bear.

Act II: Abolition
(aka the Continuation of Servitude)

The second act in the history of the engagement between Britain and the Caribbean is just about the only bit of the story which Britain tends to remember with any regularity, clarity, or enthusiasm: the abolition of slavery in Britain's colonies in 1834, following the abolition of the slave trade in its territories in 1807. Putting to one side the fact that Britain was a leader in the trade in enslaved people, and likewise in their deployment in slave labour camps, the double celebrations would have some merit if the two abolitions had delivered on their promises. But just as the celebrations of the end of the trade and of emancipation tend to overlook the preceding two hundred years in which Britain rather enthusiastically engaged in what it rather belatedly abolished, so too the celebrations are accompanied by amnesia regarding the subsequent period. It turns out that the second act, the age of abolition and beyond, is not so much a brand-new beginning as a continuation of what went before. Neither the abolition of the slave trade nor of enslavement itself fulfilled the hopes of those who most eagerly sought them.

The promise of the abolition of the slave trade rested in good part on the common-sense logic we have already mentioned—slave owners would surely learn to care for their chattels, even if they had failed to do so in the past, when those chattels could no longer be so easily and cheaply replaced. The prospect of the abolition of the trade had some perverse effects—slave owners suddenly attached a premium to obtaining young women for breeding purposes, which can hardly have been an objective of the abolitionists, for whom the harsh treatment of pregnant women was a mainstay of their arguments. Furthermore, as already mentioned, the end of the trade was only the ending of British transatlantic shipments—British ships still traded between the Caribbean islands, and plantations owners still sourced slaves, illegally, from other carriers. But the main point is that the promise of the abolition of the trade was never realized. If it ended the horrors of the Middle Passage on British vessels, it did not end the horrors of the plantations, where brutality and high mortality remained the norm, and where populations did not in fact stabilize and reproduce themselves after the end of the trade, with the exceptions (Barbados and the Bahamas) already mentioned.

If the abolition of the slave trade did not fulfil the hopes of those who advocated it, neither did the abolition of enslavement itself. As Bolland observes in a classic article, many histories of the British West Indies 'conceptualise the post-1838 colonies as "free" societies in contrast to the slave societies which preceded them. A clear distinction is rarely made between emancipation as an event…and emancipation as a human, social condition. It is too glibly assumed that the former produced the latter.'[16] But it didn't and in the hundred years after the beginning of this second act in the history between Britain and the Caribbean, Britain did not so much acquit itself of its moral debts as compound them.

Reparations were paid to slave owners for the loss of the labour of their 'chattels', but not to the slaves who had been deprived of their own labour and lives—Elizabeth Herrick's and Clarkson's voices were loudly but ineffectively raised demanding payment to the enslaved. But to make matters worse, the slaves were to be treated as unpaid 'apprentices' for six years after emancipation, thereby purchasing their own freedom while their erstwhile masters were given time to accustom themselves to the need to pay their new workers. The manifest injustice of the proposed period of unpaid labour by 'apprentices' produced opposition and the system fell by the wayside before its intended expiry date. But even with the end of apprenticeship, plantation owners in the Caribbean managed to institute forms of labour relations which lasted for more than a hundred years after emancipation and maintained patterns of work little better than slavery, both for those who had once been slaves as well as for newly imported indentured labour from south-east Asia. Nor should this outcome be seen as antipathetic to the intentions of Westminster. The devising of the apprenticeship system was the work of 'officials in the Colonial Office...struck by the need to free slaves while retaining the basic structure of plantation society in the West Indies. In their minds, one of the potential dangers for the slaves was a reversion to "barbarism" once they became free.'[17] The granting of freedom was conditional on the satisfaction of the demands of the cultivation of sugar.

Howard Johnson in his study of the economy and labour within post-emancipation period in the Bahamas, characterizes the shift as from 'slavery to servitude'. His book, he says, is an 'examination of the methods by which a white mercantile oligarchy perpetuated its social and economic control from slavery into the twentieth century'.[18] Hilary Beckles in his history of Barbados entitles his chapter covering the period 1838–1897 'Freedom without Liberties', with the first section of the chapter going under the heading 'Emancipation Betrayed'.[19] Each island had its own particular circumstances, and thus its own history—and in Jamaica, the size of the island and the ready availability of land made for the rapid creation after emancipation of a 'new class of black smallholders', mostly not reliant on labouring for a wage.[20] And yet across the region, the colonial elite generally found ways of maintaining their control over the formerly enslaved. Lack of capital or credit prevented access to land in most places; unfavourable regulation around contracts and rigorous policing of free movement inhibited anything like free bargaining for wages; the so-called 'truck system' whereby wages were paid either late or in something other than current coin, requiring workers to supply their needs by buying from their employers (at inflated prices), effectively tied people to the plantations; the encouragement of immigration, especially from the Indian sub-continent, further served to keep wages low (and, to add insult to injury, 'the high cost of importing Indians' fell heavily 'on the ex-slaves themselves through general taxation'[21]); and devices such as poll taxes denied to the newly emancipated a political voice.

Notwithstanding the degree of redistribution of land Jamaica accomplished soon after 1834, it was a Jamaican protest, the Morant Bay rebellion of 1865, which expressed the dissatisfactions and disappointments which were common to the unfree throughout the British West Indies in the period after emancipation. Concerns about wages, rents, poverty, and the grossly skewed administration of justice led to protests which were met not with understanding but with provocation. The protests grew into a rebellion, to which the governor, John Eyre, responded with the imposition of martial law and with indiscriminate brutalities against the black population, as a result of what one historian terms 'paranoia'.[22] As Eyre's successor as Governor put it, 'No one will ever believe the things that were done here in that mad bad time.'[23] Eyre's conduct was the subject of fierce controversy in Britain, but Eyre had powerful and influential defenders—chief amongst them the rabidly racist Carlyle. Though a Royal Commission judged his defence without merit, no action against him was ever successful. And it was the colonists' fears, not the discontents of the formerly enslaved, which were addressed by the British government's immediate response in the aftermath of the unrest. A Jamaican House of Assembly had sat for nearly two hundred years, its membership heavily shaped by poll taxes designed to disenfranchise all but a tiny minority of non-whites. But the very idea of representative government caused alarm to the landed elite, and the Colonial Office had the assembly stand down, and imposed direct rule from London. Even where some political rights were restored, property and other qualifications of various kinds ensured that the percentage of holders of the franchise remained astonishingly low: 5.5% in Jamaica in 1939, though lower still at 3.4% in Barbados.[24]

Emigration is a rather drastic expression of agency and protest—but it was to emigration that the unfree turned in significant numbers throughout the latter part of the nineteenth and into the early twentieth century, particularly in the economic depression of the 1880s and beyond, when malnutrition and death from starvation increased across the colonies. Early on after emancipation, Barbadians—to take one example—sought opportunities in neighbouring islands, denied land on their own island, and subject to all the inequities of a new servitude. And after 1905 many chose even hard and dangerous labour in the construction of the Panama Canal in preference to the continued slavery of the plantation.[25]

The second act of this history—the period after emancipation through to the early twentieth century—cannot then be represented as the realization of the promise of abolition, at least as that promise was conceived by the enslaved. From their perspective, the promise was not fulfilled, but (as Beckles has it) betrayed. We need to spell this out quite clearly. The British celebration of abolition not only overlooks two hundred years of British pre-eminence in the crime of transatlantic slavery, but more fundamentally still, overlooks the fact that for the enslaved, the legal act of emancipation was a moment of profound continuity, not discontinuity. Not by accident but by design, slavery's racially constructed system of exploitation continued for more than a hundred years across the Caribbean, even after slavery's supposed abolition. What we celebrate as the ending of years of gross and flagrant injustice and unfreedom was followed by years of gross and flagrant injustice and unfreedom.

The very promise of abolition was likely not quite what the enslaved took it to be. In other words, even the abolitionists didn't exactly intend freedom to mean freedom. Scanlon notes that 'ideas about the incapacity of people of African descent to govern themselves, invented by slaveholders to defend slavery, survived emancipation'[26]—though it might be more accurate to say that such ideas actually informed it. For though for some the imposition of the apprenticeship scheme and the denial of a political voice for the formerly enslaved were controversial, for many in the abolitionist camp such arrangements expressed their estimation of the enslaved.

So it was that even Britain's wider antislavery campaign in the next generation seems not so much a break with the past but its continuation by other means. The moralistic shouldering of 'the white man's burden' (and the acquisition of a vast empire), traded on this continuity: 'Britain came full circle as it carved up and despoiled Africa, conquering territories in the name of anti-slavery where Britons had once called in slave ships. The antislavery movement in the British empire had dismantled chattel slavery in Britain's colonies. But antislavery policy and rhetoric declared that by virtue of having abolished slavery, Britain had earned the right to take new colonies in the name of a civilisation that itself had been made in the crucible of the slave empire.'[27]

Act III: Colonial Neglect and Independence

The third act takes us from the early twentieth century, via the piecemeal and grudging concession of greater political and economic liberties to the peoples of the Caribbean, to the eventual independence of many long-time colonies from the 1960s onwards. Some of these islands had been held by Britain for some three hundred years, so independence represented a major change. And yet even this period of profound change is marked by continuities which add no lustre to Britain's record. The central continuity is that colonial power continued to be exercised in the interests of the metropole, white elites, and British capital, and with little regard to the interests of the colonies and their peoples—notwithstanding the official discourse of imperial mission and responsibility.[28] That the colonies should serve the interests of the colonizers was the very principle of colonization, codified into economic practices and assumptions which have become known as 'mercantilism'. But even after mercantilism had ceased to be the governing orthodoxy of political and economic practice, Britain conceived no future for the Caribbean except as a source of cheap raw materials, and as a market for British products.

As Howard Johnson tells the story, soldiers demobilized from the British West Indies Regiment after fighting for the Empire in the First World War were some of the first to experience severe disenchantment regarding 'the benevolence of British rule'. They had, notwithstanding their willingness to serve the colonial power, been subjected to 'blatant racial discrimination': 'we are treated neither as Christians nor British Citizens, but as West Indian "Niggers"', as one Trinidadian sergeant expressed it.[29] What the former soldiers had experienced was a disregard, which would determine the concluding period of direct colonial rule. London's resistance to granting responsible government to its Caribbean colonies was combined with a failure to support appropriate development.

'Despite evidence of social and economic distress'—including major periods of labour and wider unrest across the region from 1935 until the outbreak of war—colonial governments maintained a commitment to laissez-faire policy and did nothing to alleviate significantly the region's plight: 'the failure to ameliorate conditions in the British Caribbean reflects the limited responsibility which the British government accepted for colonial development'.[30] An official of the West Indian Department in the Colonial Office, arguing for establishing a commission in 1938 to report on these matters, observed that 'The West Indies, are to some extent, the British show-window for the USA—I am afraid that it is not a very striking exhibit.'[31] A Labour Member of Parliament who took a particular interest in colonial affairs throughout his career, Arthur Creech Jones, spelt it out more fully in early 1939:

> We carry a grave responsibility for a colonial policy based on cheap labour and cheap raw materials. The facts are out, and we can no longer plead ignorance and indifference. Of course, there has been official irresponsibility and the dominance of narrow calculating colonial interests. We can point to years of criminal neglect when official ineptitude and sloth have permitted affairs to drift and the islands to sink into unpardonable misery. Now a point has been reached when action is desperately urgent and British concern must be paid in hard cash. The hopeless squalor of today is in a real way the measure of the shortcomings of our colonial policy and of our economic neglect.[32]

It was, in fact, the need to impress the USA, more than any manifest concern for the islands' populations, which brought about some change, and 'the formulation of a new approach to colonial development which emphasized colonial welfare rather than metropolitan economic needs'.[33] Yet as another civil servant tartly noted in 1945 of the work of a new board focussed on the new approach, 'after four years, the use of a microscope would hardly reveal any progress on the development side in the West Indies'.[34] Industrialization was not entertained as a major objective of such modest efforts as were made—and primary products typically comprised the bulk of exports up until independence.[35]

The needs of British reconstruction after the end of war were themselves conveniently served by the plight of the colonies. The so-called Windrush generation, comprising perhaps more than 150,000 people born in the Caribbean, were drawn to Britain just because even poorly paid work in Britain was attractive to Caribbean migrants seeking to escape entrenched poverty, and its attendant ills, at home.[36] And notwithstanding that the work these migrants did was vital to the rebuilding of post-war Britain, they were met with much the same attitudes and prejudices which were shown to the soldiers of the West Indies Regiment some fifty years previously.

Meanwhile, the neglect of even the basics of development continued right up to the last days of colonial rule. The lack of provision for education immediately after emancipation had long been something of a scandal—and it was only on the eve of independence or afterwards, that provision of free secondary education became normal rather than a rarity. In 1962, Jamaican politicians asking for due support for the soon to be independent nation, pointed out to the British government that the country had secondary school places for a mere 7.5% of children of school age.[37] As Beckles puts it tellingly, at independence West Indians 'set sail on a journey to freedom and development on a turbulent ocean, in a rotting ship burdened by British debt'.[38] Britain had exited empire 'on the cheap', but not honourably.[39]

The Caribbean remains, as a result of the persistence of a 'plantation mode of production', persistently and relatively poor.[40] Present-day inhabitants still seek opportunities elsewhere—the irony being that many of the descendants of those forcibly brought to the Caribbean feel bound now to leave it. There are considerable differences between different countries: thus in 2019 Jamaica had GDP per capita of approx. $5,500, Grenada nearly $11,000, St Lucia approx. $11,500, and Barbados approx. $18,000. Measuring the wealth of nations is not without its subtleties, of course, but some feel for these numbers is given by the fact that GDP per capita of approx. $18,000 represents an average for the world. And it is worth noting too that most of the Caribbean economies, even the relatively prosperous ones, are fragile, relying very heavily on tourism and with their governments burdened by significant levels of debt. Covid hit the tourist sector with particular force: the economy of the Caribbean contracted by 8.6% in 2020 according to the World Bank, and many already delicate economies are struggling to recover.

Conclusion: Three Acts/One Story

Though I have framed the engagement between Britain and the Caribbean as a play in three acts, it might be said, to change the imagery slightly, that each seemingly new chapter reads remarkably like a continuation of the one which came before. The deepest continuity underlying the three acts of the engagement between Britain and the Caribbean is a belief in a supposed racial hierarchy. Although it was conceived in different ways at different times, this hierarchy nonetheless stood behind the periods of enslavement, servitude, and the subordination of the interests of the colonies and their inhabitants, through to modern times. There is a worthwhile enquiry regarding the relationship between enslavement and racism—specifically, it can be asked whether enslavement bred racism (which seems most likely) or whether racism led to enslavement. Either way, racism was the enabling doctrine for the crimes and wrongs of the nearly four hundred years of British dominance across much of the Caribbean world.

Johnson carefully refers to the end of the period of history he recounts as 'Constitutional Decolonization'; I take the adjective to serve as a warning that the ending of formal ties between colonial powers and their former subjects does not amount to decolonization, as such. 'Neocolonialism' was a term coined by Africans to name the continuation of colonialism by other means. So if we say that the period of Britain's engagement with the Caribbean is a story in three acts, we should not suppose that that story does not have an aftermath which somehow continues the narrative. The end of enslavement did nothing materially for a population the value of whose labour had been appropriated—misappropriated— for generations. While the purported owners of enslaved people sought and often succeeded in creating family dynasties in which wealth was harboured and enhanced over the generations, the enslaved embarked upon the new era of (un)freedom with nothing in their hands.

Relations between Britain and its Caribbean colonies followed a parallel path. The wealth which the sugar revolution created flowed to the centre and—along with the vast compensation payment which accompanied abolition—provided wealth which was not only consumed but conserved and passed on, and as deployed in the various waves of Britain's industrial revolution, generative of further wealth and prosperity. The colonies entered the post-colonial period—or the post constitutional colonial period—after centuries of subservience to the interests of the centre when their interests and development needs (including in education) had been neglected. They did not embark upon independence as empty-handed as the newly emancipated, but with chronic under-investment they entered the late twentieth century ill-equipped and ill-resourced to compete economically. More than fifty years later, at the end of the first quarter of the twenty-first century, the injustices of the past rear their head once more, as global warming poses a particular threat to low-lying tropical islands. The causes of global warming can be traced to the activities of the 'more developed economies, not least among them the old imperial powers that had built their wealth on the backs of Caribbean people'.[41] As so often in the past, even now, the benefits and burdens are not justly distributed.

It could be said that the fact of Britain's engagement in the slave trade is now widely known and acknowledged. The rather grand *Dictionary of National Biography* once occluded the significance of slavery within British society by generally preferring the term 'plantation owner' to anything more explicit.[42] The *Dictionary*, and much else, has changed. London, Bristol, and Liverpool, to take just three examples, have major museums which provide powerful exhibits documenting Britain's role in the slave trade and the sugar revolution. Similarly, the toppling of Colston from his plinth in Bristol, for all that it was a cause of controversy, did something to ensure that a major source of Bristol's wealth was no longer a secret, if ever it was. Even the National Trust, which might once have been accused of packaging a rather rosy and romantic image of Britain (fine drawing rooms, magnificent family portraits, and pleasant parkland stretching away into the distance), has got with the programme and now provides (again, not without opposition and controversy), something of the darker history of the entanglements with enslavement that so often financed the country-house idyll.

The point of this chapter, however, has been to locate the admittedly now better-known story of slavery in a wider context—such that abolition is not seen so much as a radical rupture but as very much part of a continuous narrative. The most recent children's Ladybird *British History*[43] treats slavery as something of an aberration (rather overlooking the fact that, for example, at the time of emancipation the British Army was the single largest slaveholder), and an aberration that Parliament simply put right with emancipation—as if with emancipation we were done and dusted with such unpleasantness. The focus on abolition ignores not only what was abolished but also its afterlife. It is this continuity and afterlife which means, as the next chapter will suggest, that we are not done with this history.

There is one last and important thing to say before we move on. And that is just that the story as I have told it is not *the* story of the Caribbean and its people—as if the abjection of enslavement and colonial exploitation, and the racism which underlay both, is the essence of their history. That history is rather a history of resilience, creativity, resistance, and achievement, and of the emergence of new vibrant nations from histories of oppression and neglect. It is the story, or stories, of people who crafted lives of meaning, significance, and solidarity in the face of all that aimed at frustrating or preventing such possibilities. That history is their history. The history I have told is ours more than it is theirs. And it is to the contemporary weight of that history as it bears on us that we now turn.

When History Is Not Just History

The Demands of Moral Repair

When is history not just history? When does it bear on the present in such a way as to invite, or even demand, actions in the here and now? It does so most obviously when a past wrong calls for what we might term 'moral repair'.[1]

What Is Moral Repair?

Hurts, harms, and wrongdoing threaten breaches in our relationships, and moral repair is the name we give to our usual way of attempting to protect or restore those relationships. Margaret Urban Walker notes that in everyday contexts 'we have a repertory of common moral gestures that aim at repair, such as owning up, apologizing, making amends, showing repentance, and seeking or offering forgiveness. These are the familiar everyday manoeuvres of individuals that are effective in restoring relationships after everyday wrongdoing.'[2] These gestures are deployed across a wide range of personal cases, trivial and not so trivial, from bumping into someone as we take a seat on a train, to committing a sexual infidelity. And, says Walker, they provide a basic tool kit for moral repair in the case of graver wrongs committed not only by individuals against individuals, but by institutions against individuals, by one section of society against another, and even between societies or nations.

But what, we might ask, is the logic or the form of such repair? What does it normally look like?

In extremely trivial cases, repair can be very simple indeed. If I have taken your coat from the cloakroom by mistake, and notice my error ten minutes later, simply returning it with the single word 'sorry' might well be regarded as putting things right. So too if I have inadvertently parked my car in the wrong space at work and caused you minor inconvenience. A simple apology would generally be thought adequate to put matters between us to rights. But in the case of more serious wrongdoing, something more than a simple apology will be necessary. If I have been sexually unfaithful a 'mere' sorry, as we would say, probably wouldn't cut it; nor would that do the trick if I had stolen your car; nor again if I were a doctor who had caused you harm through my negligent conduct of a medical procedure.

What more is needed in cases of more serious wrongdoing? Take that last case as an example, where a hospital's employee, through negligence, has caused major injury to a patient. What needs to happen here to accomplish moral repair? In such a case three or perhaps four elements seem to be crucial in trying to restore or repair the broken relationship. First, the hospital needs to acknowledge the wrong that has occurred—and that acknowledgment may necessitate, as a second element, attentive listening to the one who has been wronged. The wrong doer must sometimes go to some effort, with the help of the injured party, truly to fathom the wrong which has been done, if the acknowledgment is to be authentic. Thirdly, an apology needs to be offered. And then in the fourth place, some sort of recompense must be made. Moral repair will very likely fail if the hospital neglects one or other of these different elements, or simply gets one of the bits wrong.

On some occasions an acknowledgement, admission, or confession of wrongdoing may not need to be a quite separate or discrete moment in the sequence of actions which aim at moral repair. In the very simple case of the momentarily misappropriated coat, for example, the 'sorry' may in effect, contain all the admission which is needed. That I took your coat by mistake is what I am saying sorry for—and the simple sorry is at once both a confession and an expression of regret. The two moments are here perhaps elided and wrapped up in one. And in these and other simple cases, what I termed the sometimes necessary second step (allowing the wronged party to explain how they have been affected by the wrongdoing) may also seem redundant. The wrongs are of such a kind that their nature and affects are thought readily comprehensible.

Where the wrong is more substantial, however, a clear admission or confession may need to be made before the apology can be heard as exactly that—and for that admission and confession to be properly informed, the wronged party may need to express their hurt, and the offender may need to do some hard listening. We can, unfortunately, only too easily imagine a hospital writing a weasly sorry which not so much neglects as quite consciously avoids a proper confession. 'We regret', it might say, 'that the results of your recent operation were not as you would have wished them to be'. The sorry does not land, so to speak, just because there is more than a little evasion about what has really happened and who is to blame. Here, and in like cases, it behoves the maker of an apology first of all to attend to the harm which has been caused, and to be quite specific about where the blame lies. It needs to be said that the operation went wrong, the hospital needs to understand exactly what that meant for the patient, and the hospital needs to be clear that it went wrong because someone or other in the hospital was at fault (if such was the case). In childhood parlance, you have to own up before you say sorry. Children learn very quickly that saying sorry is the route to making things right—but very soon after that they also learn that their parents will not accept a mumbled and sullen 'sorry' as sufficient. 'I shouldn't have bitten my sister', 'teased the cat', 'taken the doll my brother was playing with', or whatever—these are the necessary preliminaries to an apology which can be heard. But an apology only counts if you have really attended to the hurt you have caused, are clear that you caused it, and that you regret doing so.

A confession anticipates an apology of course, and just as the apology can misfire without a confession, so a confession can misfire without an apology. The sorry, in other words, must be said since it adds something important to the confession or admission. Imagine a hospital writing to a patient admitting that the patient's loss of sight in one eye was as result of medical negligence, for which negligence they proposed to offer compensation of £25,000. We can further imagine that such a communication might be received with less than full satisfaction, even if the admission and the offer of compensation were judged adequate. The patient may just need to hear that the hospital is actually sorry for what has happened.

It is curious, perhaps, but certainly noteworthy, just how very important words can be in this context. We envisaged, a while ago, a hospital expressing 'regret' at the unfavourable and unintended outcome of an operation, but the word 'regret' may itself be heard as slightly askew in a context such as this. The point is that I can regret an outcome without being in any way personally moved or troubled by its having occurred. If the operation had gone wrong because a totally unforeseen and freak lightning storm disabled a piece of equipment, the hospital might well regret the outcome and might even say that they are sorry for it. But that regret would fall short of what is needed where there is fault, and even the sorry may not seem like the sorry which negligence or other wrongdoing demands. When I am sorry at having done something, not just at it having occurred, then I am pained by your pain. I need you to know—or rather, perhaps, you need to know—that I am genuinely moved and distressed at having caused you grief. Without being melodramatic, a genuine apology has to capture something of what the Book of Common Prayer has us say about our misdoings: 'the remembrance of them is grievous unto us, the burden of them is intolerable'. The hospital's 'regret' may seem just a little perfunctory.

Both acknowledgement and apology need to be elements in any act of moral repair which has any likelihood of achieving its goal. But there may also need to be an additional attempt to make amends. 'I will make it up to you', we say in certain cases as a postscript to the apology. How I will make it up to you will vary according to the circumstances, and for the hospital, which cannot simply undo what has gone wrong, money is likely to be deemed an appropriate means of trying to making amends.

As we have already stressed, any such making amends must normally follow an admission of responsibility, an attending to the harm done, and an expression of apology. A letter saying simply that the hospital notes the unfavourable outcome of a recent procedure and encloses a cheque for £25,000 may, as we say, 'add insult to injury'. But equally a fulsome admission of fault and a fulsome apology, unaccompanied by any further specific efforts to make amends, may be construed as a cynical attempt to move on a bit too quickly and without facing up to what taking responsibility entails. The delicacy lies, of course, in identifying the right mode of making amends, and if money is that mode, the right amount.

In the case of the negligent hospital, money might be an expected way of trying to address the wrong—but £100 won't do it for sure. The question of what is the right amount is unlikely to be a question which admits of a precise answer, in this or in more complex cases, so some sensitivity and willingness to explore the issue would seem to be a prerequisite to identifying a sum which may be judged appropriate by all sides.

There are, however, plenty of cases where money is exactly not the means of fulfilling the promise 'I will make it up to you.' Even where money is part of the solution, it may be thought of as simply the best we can do, without there being any pretence that it puts everything back to rights. But there are cases where the very offer of money will seem wrong—so if moral repair typically requires our making amends, the character of that making is quite various. Or to put it more bluntly, an offer of £25,000 should not accompany a confession of and apology for a sexual infidelity.

Clearly, apart from in the most trivial cases, moral repair is a work which calls for a certain finesse. It is possible to get each of the elements wrong—the acknowledgment, the listening which may need to inform that acknowledgment, the apology, and the making amends—and it is also possible to put them together ineptly. But alongside the hazards involved in the attempt, we need also to admit, as Walker does, that there is nothing to say that every situation created by moral wrongdoing can be repaired. It cannot be asserted that acknowledgment, apology, and making amends are together always sufficient to accomplish such a repair. But what can be said is that full and honest acknowledgments, heartfelt apologies, and sensitive attempts at understanding the harms done and making amends, provide the best possible chance of repair.

There is, certainly in cases of grave misdoing, no panacea which somehow wipes the slate clean. But Walker's modest conclusion is surely right:

> If no wrongs can be fully righted as no bell can be unrung, there is still plenty of room for reparative gestures that work on the moral plane to relieve suffering, disillusionment, isolation and despair. Too little is better than nothing, and small gestures can carry larger meanings or can be a starting point for a broader reconsideration of relationships between individuals and within societies. The refusal of even the small gesture, on the other hand, can feed bitterness, rage and despair.[3]

When History Is Not Done With

Moral repair is a means by which we address the wrongs of the past. The last chapter suggested that the history which has occurred between Britain and the Caribbean is a dark and painful history of wrongdoing, stretching over some 350 years, and with ongoing consequences on both sides. So here we have a case where we ought to consider whether and how we can address this particular shared past by means of moral repair. The discussion so far suggests what that might look like. In the first place, Britain would need to document and acknowledge the depth and extent of its entanglements with the Atlantic trade in enslaved people and with the deathly sugar revolution which it served, and with its later legacies. Secondly this would also necessitate a real effort to listen to voices from the past and present, who can most tellingly describe the suffering which this revolution caused and continues to cause. It would need, thirdly, to find a way of appropriately expressing the regret and sorrow which a proper knowledge of this history would evince. And in the fourth place, Britain would need to explore the possibility of trying to repair the damage which has been done, perhaps by way of reparations.

Of course, there are lots of questions and objections which may arise at this point—and we are going to come to those objections in the next few chapters. In my experience, however, it is quite extraordinary how triggering for some that word 'reparations' is. I imagine (I hope not wishfully), that what I have been discussing thus far in this chapter seems like rather homely common sense. Most of us have a fairly reliable grasp of the social conventions and expectations which enable us to overcome the intended and unintended injuries we cause one another and which threaten to cause breaches in our relationships. And we have a good sense of how what works in the smaller and more intimate spaces of family and friendship, may, in a slightly different key, work in the larger and more impersonal spaces of wider social interactions. There are no radical thoughts or big surprises here. But mention the word 'reparations' and temperatures and tempers seem to rise. And I have got used at this point in talks and discussions to be being denounced as 'woke'.

The word 'woke' has been subject to what is referred to in linguistics as 'pejoration'—that is, it has gone from being a positive to being a negative (or pejorative) term. Once upon a time being woke was a good thing, as the injunction 'stay woke' indicated. To be woke in this sense was to be aware of the social injustices which for African Americans who used the phrase, were not matters of abstract inequity but of personal endangerment. Now, however, the word is used more often negatively than positively, as a term of abuse. As with other abusive terms, it is somewhat easier to recognize that those who fling it around are registering disapproval than to determine where precisely their disapproval lies. But the gist of it seems to be that to be woke is to be faddishly concerned, and over concerned, with issues around identity, discrimination, and injustice. Even before one gets into any specifics, the very idea that reparations might have a role in addressing the history between Britain and the Caribbean seems to evoke an accusation of wokeness—as if, that is, it expresses some contemporary excessive sensitivities around trauma and wrongdoing.

But where, we might ask, does the idea of reparations come from? Many of us, scratching our heads at this point, can probably reach back to history lessons at school and call to mind the Versailles Treaty of 1919. For advocates of reparations, it is a rather unhappy example—the burden of reparation payments placed on Germany is commonly recognized as one of the causes of the social resentments and political malaise which led to the rise of Hitler. But perhaps this example is beside the point, since any sense of the faddishness of seeking reparations doesn't relate to the notion of seeking reparations in relation to war, a practice which has some pedigree. It is rather, so it seems, the wider application of the idea of reparations which provokes disdain, once we move outside that very specific context. And yet—here is the point—one quite important source of the idea of reparations does allow for such wider application and goes back far enough to dispel the notion that the idea is simply some shallow trend of the moment.

Dredging up history lessons is hard enough. Dredging up RE (= Religious Education) or even Sunday School lessons, may be a bigger ask. But many people remember the story of Zacchaeus, the tax gatherer who was long in funds but short in stature. What makes him especially memorable, perhaps, is just that his solution to the problem of his lack of height—he climbed a tree to get a better view of Jesus from above the crowd—was something that any normal child would probably have preferred to be doing over against sitting in a classroom listening to a teacher banging on. That is by the way, however. More to the point: when Jesus calls Zacchaeus down from his perch, 'Zacchaeus stood and said to the Lord, "Behold, Lord, the half of my goods I give to the poor; and if I have defrauded any one of anything, I restore if fourfold." '[4] To this declaration Jesus responds with the ringing endorsement: 'Today salvation has come to this house.'

What Zacchaeus says and does is exactly exemplary of the form of moral endeavour which we have been terming 'moral repair'. The threefold form of his action is perhaps not immediately transparent, since there is no explicit spoken apology. But his standing and saying is clearly a public and open acknowledgment or confession of his misdoings. His promise of fourfold return to any he may have defrauded is manifestly a generous bid to make amends. And the sorry, although not said out loud, is surely encompassed in the words and gesture—just as, in a different context, a bunch of flowers says sorry without any words being spoken. (If there is any complaint to be made, it might be that Zacchaeus would provide a better model if he showed a concern to understand the depth of harm he may have done.)

Now the biblical text does not use the term 'reparations' to describe what Zacchaeus commits to—in fact it only tells us what he does without providing any labels for, or analysis of it. But preaching two sermons on this text, a seventeenth-century Archbishop of Canterbury, John Tillotson, uses the very term 'reparation'. The sermons are put together under the title 'On the Nature and Necessity of Restitution'.[5] And restitution, Tillotson tells us, 'is nothing else but the making of reparation or satisfaction to another for the injuries we have done him. It is to restore a man to the condition from which, contrary to right and to our duty, we have removed him.' As to what sort of injuries these may be, Tillotson mentions different kinds, including injuries 'either by fraud and cunning, or by violence and oppression: either by overreaching another man in wit, or overbearing him by power.' As to how restitution, or reparation is to be made, it can be in kind or in value—or where 'the value … is not certain, we are to give reasonable satisfaction'.

In the cool and analytic terms of seventeenth-century moral thought, taking a biblical text for his guide, Tillotson commends to us—to go back to Walker's terms—'moral repair'. As we move forward to ask what moral repair might look like specifically in relation to the wrongdoings which constitute the history of the Caribbean under British rule, we can be sure of one thing. And that is that the charge that the idea of making reparation in cases of grave wrong doing is woke, meaning 'faddishly trendy', is wrong. Or at least, if it is right, both Zacchaeus and Tillotson were way ahead of their times.

4

Eleven (Mostly Not Very Good) Objections to Reparations

Introduction

In the last two chapters I have tried to outline the historical and moral basis for the claim that Britain owes reparations to the Caribbean. The historical case is founded on the wrongs of enslavement and colonialism, through which riches flowed to Britons and to Britain, leaving the countries of the region poor and underdeveloped even down to the present day. The moral case is simple, and not founded on any deep or complex moral theories, but on everyday ethical practices. When we have wronged one another, in ways great or small, what is asked of us is what we have been terming moral repair, typically comprising acknowledgment, attending to the grief and grievances of those we have harmed, apology, and making amends. Moral repair and reparations (in the widest sense of the term), are surely then due from the UK to the Caribbean.

At the end of that last chapter we briefly considered the rather flimsy objection that the very idea of reparations is 'woke'. In my experience, however, there are a host of objections that don't necessarily dismiss reparations out of hand, but which attend to specific details of the historical or moral circumstances between Britain and the Caribbean and allege that in view of these very details and circumstances, moral repair is unnecessary or inappropriate. Whenever I have spoken or written on the topic, pretty much the same set of complaints and cavils can be relied on to turn up in discussion—and I have tried to capture them point by point in what follows. Each of these objections deserves a hearing. Some of them, however, are only a little less flimsy than the charge of 'wokery'; others are altogether more weighty. Considering them one by one will help us clarify some vexed issues around intergenerational responsibility, guilt, and shame, as well as allowing us to acknowledge the limits of what reparations can be expected to achieve.

'It's a Long Time Ago—Time to Move On'

A friend visiting me in Cambridge from another university once told me a story about the delicate manners of my colleagues. He had, on a previous occasion, had dinner in my college (Trinity), when the conversation had turned to music. A particular Beethoven sonata was mentioned. 'I vividly remember hearing the strains of that sonata drifting across the court from your rooms to mine one summer's evening, it must have been more than twenty years ago now', said one elderly Fellow to another. 'I do so hope I didn't disturb you', was the earnest reply.

History does not record how this somewhat belated apology was received at the time, but we are supposed to laugh. To be concerned whether you may inadvertently have mildly disturbed someone twenty years ago suggests an unusually and overly sensitive conscience. Equally, looking at it from the other side, if the person who may have been very mildly disturbed had, twenty years on, demanded an apology, or grumbled that the one proffered was not good enough, we would be inclined to judge them over sensitive in a different way—'resentful', 'rancorous', and 'grudging' are words which come to mind. Both the passage of time, and the lightness of the offence (if there was one), make the giving of the apology somewhat comic—and any insistence on it absurdly or excessively touchy.

Now manifestly the wrongs of slavery and colonialism don't fall into the same category as regards gravity of the offence. On the other hand, however, slavery is not twenty years in the past, but, at least between Britain and the Caribbean, nearly two hundred years in the past. And two hundred years, it might be said, really does amount to a quantity of time sufficient for the popular maxim to apply which asserts that 'time heals all'. So, isn't it indeed just time to forget and move on?

There is an important point here, though this is not the place to explore it in great depth. It is that forgetting and moving on most certainly do have a place in the context of moral repair. The word 'amnesty' is related to the word 'amnesia'—and an amnesty is a sort of brokered forgetting. Thought of like that, an amnesty is a little way away from moral repair. Under an amnesty everyone agrees to a cessation of hostilities, perhaps out of mere weariness and a wish to get back to normal life—even if there has been no reconciliation in any fractured relationships. But even if an amnesty is a step away from moral repair, forgetting may have its place even where moral repair is attempted and occurs—indeed, 'let's forget about it' is a regular formula used, typically by a wronged party, to signal that a proffered apology or other attempt at making amends is indeed enough to put things right, or even above and beyond what's required.

Now just as there can be a failure on the part of those who owe moral repair, so there can be a failure on the part of those to whom it is owed. The failures on the one side we have already mentioned—the failures to confess, understand the harm they have caused, to apologize, or try to make things right in appropriate, thoughtful, and sensitive ways. But there are indeed failures on the other side, on the side of those to whom repair is owed. The likely failure here will be a failure to acknowledge and accept what can reasonably be expected or required by way of amends, or to acknowledge—in our trivial example of the wafting piano music— that the offence was small and in the rather dim and distant past.

So, 'it's time to forget and move on' is not an illegitimate thought in the context of dealing with historical injustices and wrong doings. There are, however, a number of points that are important when judging the appeal to such notions in relation to the question of what Britain may or may not owe the Caribbean:

i. The objection misses an important aspect of the situation—most obviously it overlooks the fact that, as we have argued in Chapter 2, Britain did not turn over a new leaf at emancipation, but found new ways of unjustly extracting value from its colonies, right down to modern times. 'It all happened a long time ago' isn't obviously true.

ii. More to the point, the time in which wrongs may be expected to heal of themselves, so to speak, is a function of the depth of the wrongs in question as well as of the length of time since they occurred—and the wrongs of slavery and colonialism are grave and deep and reach into the present. To put it another way, unlike the case of the possible sound pollution caused by the mildly intrusive Beethoven sonata, slavery and colonialism constitute not so much a wrong, but a wound, the effects of which are arguably felt day after day, year after year, generation after generation.

iii. 'Let's forget about it' is, of course, best and usually said by the wronged party, not by those who might be expected to make some sort of satisfaction. So in any discussion of reparations in the context of transatlantic slavery, such a comment can't really come from this side of the Atlantic.

iv. It has to be conceded, nonetheless and just to complete the point, that there are some circumstances where 'it's time to move on' can be said even by the side who owe reparations—but surely only in very particular contexts where that side has demonstrably gone to great lengths to say and do the right thing. But that is not the situation between Britain and the Caribbean. Given how things stand, and given Britain's failure to acknowledge, attend, apologize, or make amends, 'time to move on' said now from the British side would actually amount to an opening gambit. As such it would be a wilful refusal to face up to the issues.

General maxims are generally telling. We wouldn't rely on them unless they provided useful rules of thumb. But in relation to the history that occurred between Britain and the Caribbean, 'Time heals all' or 'Time to move on' sounds glib or even callous, especially when said from the side of Britain, not from the Caribbean—a matter of sweeping it under the carpet, as we say. Enslavement and colonialism were wrongs of the greatest gravity, the effects of which persist even after both have officially come to an end.

'Everyone Thought Slavery Was Morally Acceptable Back Then. Standards Change, but There Is No Reason for Us to Apologise or Seek to Make Amends in Our Day for What Was Thought Unexceptional at the Time. This Is to Judge the Past from the Present'

This is a very common thought, but it seems to me to be problematic from a number of angles.

First, let's grant the premise—even though it's false, or at the very least, somewhat misleading. That is, let's allow for the sake of argument that everyone did think slavery was morally acceptable back then. The point is that even if we allow this to be true for moment, it is not at all clear that it forbids us from taking up a critical position in relation to the past, or argues against us needing to make reparations.

In the second place, however, we need to challenge the premise. It is just not the case that everyone thought slavery was acceptable. On the contrary, there was a vocal and prominent critique of slavery for a very long period prior to abolition. The West Indian Interest who battled to the last to protect their position and to preserve enslavement were not unaware of the vigorously stated and widely disseminated objections to slavery. They simply preferred to ignore them.

But for the moment let's go with the thought that slavery was simply acceptable in the eighteenth century—or perhaps it would be better to say that it was, morally speaking, somewhat unremarkable or 'ordinary', to use Donington's word.[1] It can certainly be hard for us, with our sensibilities, to grasp the fact that many who were engaged in the slave trade in one way or another were not simply rapacious immoralists, devoid of a moral conscience (though some were). Edward Colston, of falling statue fame, is a case in point. His name was, and is slightly less so now, memorialized across the city of Bristol, not because of his great wealth, but because he applied that wealth generously to numerous and diverse charitable purposes. Less celebrated, but all the more telling for being rather more routine, is the example of a group of eighteenth-century London merchants, among whom a certain Richard Oswald was a leading light.[2]

The author of a study of these twenty-three merchants names them 'Citizens of the World', for though being somewhat outsiders to the City of London, they nonetheless forged successful careers by managing trading networks which spanned the globe. Their businesses had diverse components—but the hinge around which this network operated was a slave trading post on Bance Island in the mouth of the Sierra Leone River, and the plantations in the West Indies which this trading post supplied. Oswald, the leading figure amongst this association, showed a certain and by no means common concern for his captives: 'he once ordered his captains to ignore international custom [and] forgo branding slaves with hot irons....Later he ordered his Florida overseers to keep slave families from Bance Island together on the same plantation.' But for all that, Hancock concludes, 'A proprietor of the day valued slaves' productivity over their happiness and liberty.

Sitting in his faraway London counting house, Oswald did not think a great deal about the inhumanity. He expressed concern from time to time, but nonetheless he allowed himself to be distanced and dissociated from the non-commercial aspects of slaving.'[3]

But—and here's what we need to notice—for all that Oswald and his associates' global trading empire traded on inhumanity, he and his associates were men of a philanthropic disposition. Oswald and the others regularly gave to the poor of their parishes, and supported, amongst other charitable foundations, hospitals for foundlings, the sick in general, for those with smallpox, and for poor women lying in, as well as a house for penitent prostitutes.

So yes, it is true, to a certain extent, that slavery was seemingly found uncontroversial by otherwise respectable, and indeed charitable, individuals—or just to put it in the terms we imagined our objector stating it, 'slavery was morally acceptable back then'.

But what, we might wonder, really follows from this? The point of the objection is to say that the unremarkable status of slavery at the time, closes the door on any contemporary discussion of reparations. But a moment's reflection allows us to see that such a conclusion is, at the very least, problematic. Take two examples where we would immediately sense a difficulty.

British boarding schools in the 1960s, '70s and even later, were notoriously tolerant of what would now be identified as sexual abuse of children. A headmaster of the most prestigious public school in the country was celebrated as a truly great headmaster, even while his predilections (to use the euphemism of the time) were—hush, hush—widely known. To speak more generally, even when complaints made against masters (it was usually men) became too frequent and loud to ignore, the normal thing was to help the offender slip into another job at a similar establishment—after all, it would be said, he was probably rather good at teaching the boys maths or whatever, and it would be a pity to see his career end abruptly and scandalously.

So things were handled at the time. It is hard to see, however, that because such behaviour was tolerated or winked at at the time, it would be improper now to judge what happened then as a dreadful wrong. Nor does it seem to preclude our taking appropriate steps in the here and now to try to address those wrongs and the suffering they caused—perhaps by removing the offending headmaster's portrait from the dining hall, apologizing to the victims, and even making payments in recognition of the suffering endured, for example. (And many schools in the UK have reached settlements with former pupils in recent years—twenty, thirty, or more years after offences were committed, notwithstanding that at the time when occurred, the offences were judged less critically, and often regarded as little more than minor misdemeanours.)

The objector we have been imagining might just cry 'foul' here. The analogy is, like all analogies, good as far as it goes—but there are important dissimilarities between this example and the case of enslavement. The most obvious one is just that though the 'predilections' were winked at, they weren't simply acceptable either. Our eighteenth-century merchant with a commercial interest in slavery probably wouldn't have felt any need to conceal that interest; not so the headmaster and the other masters. So our modern case is not an example of the propriety of judging the past by standards from the present—the fact that the headmaster and the master liked to keep things 'hush hush' shows that they themselves knew that what was going on was thought to be dodgy, at least by others, even if they may have tried to justify it to themselves.

But let's take a different example. Discrimination against, and even persecution of, the Jews was very widely accepted in Germany in the 1930s—not only accepted, but regarded as commendable and patriotic. Surely here, whatever we say about the exact shape and character of public sentiment on this issue, the greater its uniformity the more sinister it becomes. That is to say the lack of voices raised in opposition to the persecution does not make things better, but rather worse. And it seems to me that we would not be in the least inclined to take general approval of a programme of persecution as meaning that any contemporary case for moral repair would fall by the wayside. It would seem very odd indeed to suggest that a current case for reparations should fail just because there was no opposition to what is complained of back in the day.

We were, however, only granting the premise for the sake of argument. The fact is that the simple assertion that slavery was generally held to be morally acceptable is at worst simply false, but in any case, highly misleading.

It is worth noting in the first place that slavery was nearly always held to be a terrible affront when it happened to people like us. The Trinitarian Order (more fully, the Order of the Most Holy Trinity for the Redemption of Captives) was founded in France in 1198 and was devoted to ransoming Christian slaves held by Muslims across the Middle East, North Africa and Spain. The Mercedarians (or the Royal, Celestial and Military Order of our Lady of Mercy and the Redemption of the Captives) were established some twenty years later with much the same mission, in Barcelona, on the very frontline of Christian/Muslim encounter.

The irony is, of course, that these orders were still going strong ransoming Christian victims of enslavement some 250 years later—just as the first Africans enslaved by Europeans were becoming an established element in Spanish society, comprising perhaps 10% of the population in such major urban centres as Seville at the end of the fifteenth century.

So perhaps we need to modify the claim: perhaps what is meant is that the enslavement of *Africans* was held to be generally acceptable. But again, even that claim requires some nuance.

In passing we should notice the early Quaker critiques of slavery, from the 1670s onwards. The general view of Quakers as wild radicals meant, perhaps, that for all the force and clarity of Fox's denunciations of what he observed in Barbados, they were easily overlooked—and even the Quakers themselves remained divided on the issue of slavery for close on another ninety years. It was only in 1761 that British Quakers excluded from their society any of their fellows connected with the trade. Fox indeed tended to complain of the treatment of slaves, rather than directly objecting to the very institution of slavery—though it is striking that the basis of his complaints to Anglican ministers who neglected to teach or minister to the enslaved harped on a theme that would be the bedrock of the later abolitionist campaigns: 'Is not the Gospel to be preached to all Creatures? And are not they Creatures? And did not Christ taste death for every man? And are they not Men?'[4]

From 1748 onwards Montesquieu and other figures of the French enlightenment attacked slavery directly and head on. The two Adams of the Scottish enlightenment, Ferguson and Smith, followed suit within twenty years. Evangelicals, in the footsteps of the Quakers, were joining in the protest in the early 1770s, and most influentially of all, John Wesley's *Thoughts upon Slavery* of

1774, enjoyed wide circulation, and declared slavery a 'violation of justice, mercy and truth'.[5]

Perhaps more significant, however, is to notice not the voices of intellectuals, radicals, and dissenters—whose views, then, as now, would probably come with the serving suggestion, 'add a large pinch of salt'. Samuel Johnson, of dictionary fame, was a staunchly Tory and conservative figure, and yet consistently outspoken in his opposition to slavery. Less celebrated, but equally noteworthy is William Paley, an Anglican clergyman, who, in his own lifetime and beyond, was regarded as a pillar of religious orthodoxy and the establishment. Paley was certainly not woke—his pamphlet entitled 'Reasons for Contentment: Addressed to the Labouring Part of the British Public', contains such gems as the observation that 'Frugality itself is a pleasure'. (History does not seem to record how grateful or otherwise were the labouring part of the British Public for his counsel.) It is all the more striking, then, to find this undoubted member of the religious and social establishment attacking slavery in 1785 with a brevity and emphasis which seems to suppose that the case against this 'wickedness' brooks no serious contention.

The enslaved, he writes, are shipped to the Americas 'with no more accommodation... than what is provided for brutes'; in the colonies 'the miserable exiles' are subject, 'for life', to 'a dominion and system of laws, the most merciless and tyrannical that ever were tolerated upon the face of the earth'; and the 'inordinate authority' conferred upon the slave holder is 'exercised with rigour and brutality'. And how is such 'abominable tyranny', this 'odious institution', typically excused? 'It is said, that it [the colonial plantation] could not be cultivated with quite the same convenience and cheapness, as by the labour of slaves: by which means, a pound of sugar which the planter now sells for sixpence, could not be afforded under sixpence halfpenny.'[6] Or as Cowper put it in a poem published three years later:

> I own I am shock'd at the purchase of slaves,
> And fear those who buy and sell them are knaves,
> What I hear of their hardships, their tortures and groans,
> Is almost enough to draw pity from stones.
> I pity them greatly, but I must be mum,
> For how could we do without sugar and rum?

It should not be thought that such judgements on enslavement were those of elite scholars (and poets) alone. In 1787, two years after Paley was writing, 10,000 people in Manchester (a city which benefited from the triangular trade), signed a petition against the slave trade—and they paid for advertisements in newspapers across Britain to tell others of their initiative.[7] 'By the time of the 1788 session of Parliament adjourned', reports Adam Hochschild, '103 petitions for abolition or reform of the slave trade had been signed by between 60,000 and 100,000 people.'[8] In 1789, 769 metalworkers from Sheffield petitioned Parliament against the slave trade—even though their livelihood depended on the shipment of knives, scissors, scythes, and the like to West Africa (some of the most popular of the English manufactured goods to be traded for kidnapped Africans).[9] Petitions were just one element in the widespread popular campaigning and agitation, which were important aspects of the abolitionists' activities, alongside the regular and routine work inside Parliament—women were especially active in the movement and widely supported such measures as the boycotting of slave-grown sugar. All in all, the abolitionist movement, as Hochshild puts it, quickly took on 'a highly democratic flavour'.[10]

Petitions, poetry, polemics, and even paintings were deployed in the abolitionist cause, such that 'by the 1780s', concludes one historian, 'the intellectual argument against slavery had been won, in that it was no longer generally regarded as defensible on grounds other than material expediency'.[11]

It would be tempting—but mistaken—to conclude that all that Wilberforce, Clarkson, et al. had to do was to join the dots, so to speak. For as Christopher Leslie Brown appositely puts it, there is something of a 'chasm' between 'moral opinion' and 'moral action'.[12] The beginning of the focussed campaign against the slave trade, from which the movement for the abolition of slavery would in turn flow, is generally dated to a meeting in 2 George Yard in the City of London, in May 1787 (two years after Paley's quick fire denunciation of slavery). But the first campaign would last nearly twenty years and the second another twenty years again.

But here's the point. The arguments against enslavement, however they were embellished, developed, or reinforced in those forty years of campaigning, were not new to the stage. Far from it. For more than ninety years before the curtain fell on 'this odious institution', arguments against enslavement were very widely disseminated, well known and accepted by high and low. It is simply misleading, then, to think that one can describe this state of affairs with the little line, 'slavery was morally unexceptional back then'. The 45,000 or so claimants on the register of compensation at the time of emancipation, owning some 650,000 enslaved people, were not unacquainted with moral reservations regarding slavery. They simply chose to look the other way—or rather, in many cases, to fight to the bitter end against change. Even after the Emancipation Act was passed, the colonies, which needed to enact its provisions for themselves, only 'fell into line' when it was made clear that 'compensation would not be paid' until they had indeed enacted the relevant provisions. Prior to that the Jamaican House of Assembly 'toyed with rejecting the Act altogether'.[13]

There is, however, one feature of the lives of plantation owners themselves that tells us, I think, that even before the height of the controversy over slavery they did not all necessarily quite believe what their latter-day defenders foist upon them. It was a common practice for young merchants and planters sent out to the Caribbean to take—the word 'take' is the right one, of course—mistresses from amongst their 'chattels'. These alliances, naturally enough, often resulted in children. But with fortunes made on their plantations in their pockets, these men would often later contract more advantageous and respectable marriages. And yet, in some cases, the women and children from the earlier life were not simply forgotten, whatever new ties were formed. And many a will written by a slave owner makes provision for these women and children (after provision for the 'proper' family), sometimes specifically by way of emancipation.

A certain George Williams, who is somewhat difficult to identify—there being thirteen different individuals with the surname Williams in the relevant Jamaican records of landholdings—seems not to have made any later more socially acceptable and advantageous alliance. But in his will, proved in Jamaica in 1775, he manumitted and gave annuities to three of his female slaves: Queen (a 'negro'), Fanny Douglass ('mulatto'), and Jenny Webb (also 'mulatto'). To his nine children (two daughters and seven sons), variously 'begotten by me on the body of my negro woman slave named Quasheba otherwise Queen', 'begotten on the body of my sambo woman slave named Amelia', or 'begotten on the body of my mulatto woman slave named Fanny Douglas', he left various sums, manumitting the seven sons.[14] The daughters, perhaps, had already been freed—maybe their father feared that they might be subject to the sexual coercion of enslaved women which was, as he well knew, routine on the plantation.

What should we make of such post mortem concern expressed by slave-holders for the women and children of their irregular alliances? It suggests, of course, that even bonds formed in bondage could come to possess sentimental value to slavery's practitioners, even if the very forming of those bonds transgressed and subverted the harsh racist assumptions on which the institution relied. But doesn't the emancipation of their progeny also suggest that even slave-holders did not quite embrace the thought which is supposed to block the way to reparations and from which we set out—that slavery was morally unexceptionable?

'Slavery Was Legal Back Then, So There Can Be No Question of Making Amends for It Now'

This claim, mirroring the one about morals, serves as something of a fall-back position. The case that slavery was morally acceptable back then could fail, and yet this claim might still be thought to defeat any case for reparations. Okay, someone might say— perhaps slave owners may be judged less than morally sensitive, but what they were doing was legal. And though 'it's legal' may be a less inspiring defence than 'it's ethical', it is still a defence.

Some years ago, when I was engaged with the world of environmental policy and regulation and somewhat overwhelmed by the veritable swamp of acronyms (think COP, EPA, IPPC, NOx, SOx,

NFFO, and so on), someone introduced me to the less well known CATNIP. It stands for Cheapest Action That will Not Incur Prosecution. A company adopting CATNIP as its general modus operandi will certainly not win any environmental plaudits, but as long as it stays on the right side of the line, it won't find itself having to pay anyone damages. (And said company, if it sought to endow a wing of an art gallery, or a new lecture theatre in a university, would probably find its money proved quite acceptable, thank you.) At the time of the bicentenary of the abolition of the slave trade, Tony Blair expressed his 'deep sorrow' for Britain's role, describing it as 'profoundly shameful'—and, as he noted, 'It is hard to believe that what would now be a crime against humanity was legal at the time.'[15] But though it may be hard to believe, the line 'it was legal at the time' is considered by some, perhaps including Mr Blair, to foreclose any argument for reparations.

Just as the claim about slavery being legal mirrors the claim about it being moral, so, I think, our answer to this claim can mirror our answer to the last. In other words, the premise is, if not simply false, not simply and evidently true. Furthermore, even were it true, it is by no means clear that it blocks any argument for redress.

Take then the simple claim that slavery was legal. Any such claim needs to be hedged about with a host of qualifications.

The legal framework around slavery was 'underdeveloped' in England, as Draper puts it—if not under colonial law. The deepest irony is that 'Only with the passage of the Abolition Act itself did the British Parliament directly address the legality of colonial slavery, sanctioning "property in men" through the provision of compensation' at the very time 'it was striking down such ownership'.[16] Of course slavery was not prohibited until the passing of this Act, but neither was it positively endorsed by statute. The slave-owning Lord Vincent 'inadvertently highlighted' the fact of slavery's only indirect recognition, when, in a Parliamentary debate, he took himself to be recounting the security of this recognition—'he drew sequentially upon an act of William III that exempted the importation of Negroes from duty; two acts under George III that dealt with mortgage law; and the Act establishing slave-registers'.[17] The establishment of the registers on which he relied was, of course, a measure promoted by abolitionists.

Slavery was noticed in passing in English law, then, not so much straightforwardly recognized and endorsed in explicit terms. And it was this state of affairs which allowed for Lord Chief Justice Mansfield's famously 'Delphic'[18] judgement in the Somerset case of 1772, concerning a runaway slave captured in London and returned to his master to be shipped back to Jamaica. Mansfield declared that the state of slavery is 'so odious, that nothing can be suffered to support it, but positive law'. On this basis he ruled that 'the black must be discharged' meaning that, on English soil, no slave owner had the security of possession he or she took for granted in the colonies. Mansfield's judgement was variously interpreted, but it did not exactly abolish slavery in Britain, and certainly not in the Caribbean, even if some at the time welcomed it on those terms. And yet, in the light of Mansfield's ruling, even the arch-apologist for the West Indian interest, Edward Long, conceded that slavery was, as he put it, 'repugnant to the spirit of the English laws'[19]—as had been the conclusion of William Blackstone, the leading English jurist of the eighteenth century, in his immensely influential four volume *Commentaries on the Laws of England*, published between 1765 and 1769.

It is said that Mansfield's ruling in the Somerset case shortly afterwards (in 1778) inspired Joseph Knight, a man who had been bought in Jamaica by John Wedderburn—who brought him back to Scotland as his slave. When Wedderburn refused to allow Knight to live with his wife and child or children, Knight left his service but was arrested. The Justices of the Peace found for Wedderburn. Knight successfully appealed to the Sheriff, but Wedderburn appealed in turn to Edinburgh's Court of Session, the highest authority. The Court of Session, by an eight to four majority, confirmed the Sheriff's judgement that 'the state of slavery is not recognised by the laws of this Kingdom, and is inconsistent with the principles thereof'. Or as the most distinguished and learned of the twelve judges, Lord Kames, put it more pithily: 'we sit here to enforce right not to enforce wrong'.[20]

So—'it was legal back then'—though not perhaps plainly false, ignores something of the ambivalent status of slavery in English and in Scottish law. But that, we might say, is by the way, since, as with the moral case, we may grant the premise for the sake of argument and still think the conclusion (that there can be no case for reparations) dubious.

Allow for the sake of argument then that slavery was legal—without any of the severe qualifications that actually need to hedge about that claim. The fact of such legality does not, however, end the argument. In the indictment filed by the prosecutors at the Nuremburg trials in October 1945, 'enslavement' was identified as a crime against humanity, along with murder, extermination, deportation, and so on. It was acknowledged, at the very same time, that no such offence could be said to have existed previous to the trial. Enslaving peoples was not, then, illegal in 1939 in reference to any existing code. The Nuremburg trial proceeded on

the basis, however, that enslaving peoples as a mode of conducting war or international relations was illegitimate, no matter the
state of positive law. Just such a view was current, and even commonplace, in eighteenth- and nineteenth-century England.
Opponents of chattel slavery regularly referred to slavery in
debates in the House of Lords and the Commons as not only a sin
but a crime. As the Duke of Devonshire put it rather acidly: 'I consider the claims of the West Indian to compensation, if his property were destroyed, as the claim of a Receiver of stolen goods.'[21]

So maybe it was, in a manner of speaking, legal back then—but,
as the Allies concluded in 1945, that isn't a bar to claims for redress
in the case of egregiously grave wrongs.

And one final thought in relation to this line of thinking. It is
obviously the case that if slavery was in some sense deemed
legal in the eighteenth century, it was chiefly so in the eyes of its
perpetrators, not in the eyes of its victims, and the perpetrators
made their own rules. Looked at from this perspective, the
insistence on slavery's legality seems little better than answering a charge of injustice by saying 'we make the rules'. And, as
we have already had cause to note, the rules were not made
from some disinterested perspective, but from a deeply preju-
diced one. Once upon a time what is now deemed rape (such as
nonconsensual sex between a husband and wife) was perfectly
acceptable in the eyes of many husbands and of the law—but
we name the perspective from which that judgement was made
'patriarchy', meaning by that an ideology (in a pejorative sense)
which explains and justifies the domination of men over women
through a variety of myths and prejudices. The perspective
from which slavery was legal was racism and its associated
mythologies.

Edward Long, an enslaver in Jamaica, and a leading apologist for enslavement (especially in his *History of Jamaica* of 1774), bases his apology on Africans being the lowest 'species' of humanity. Converting Africans to Christianity was a doomed project, because of their 'barbarous stupidity'.[22] So yes, some did indeed judge enslavement legal. But the ground on which they stood is not ground any would now wish to claim in denying the case for reparations.

'Africans Sold Africans—Why Should We Take the Blame?'

Slavery was current in Africa prior to the arrival of the Portuguese and other western powers, and African slavers were often the middle men in the Atlantic slave trade. These sometimes seem to be thought very weighty truths by those who are minded to excuse Europeans.

Slavery took two forms in Africa prior to, and indeed alongside, the Atlantic trade. A trans-Saharan trade took mainly women to the Middle East, and was many years old when the Portuguese arrived.[23] But there was also within Africa what one might term indigenous slavery, also with a long history and which, according to some accounts, solved a problem analogous to the problem that faced planters in the Caribbean—abundant land and few people. With whatever underlying economic or other logic, however, many African kingdoms sold and bought people, often over long distances.[24]

It is difficult to see, however, that these facts bear very much on the matter of reparations. Europeans were not the sole originators of the practice of enslaving people, and it may be true of some of the initial trades in the opening up of the Atlantic routes, that others would have purchased the 'goods' if the Portuguese, let us say, had not. (Though try using that as an excuse for knowingly buying a stolen car and see how far you get.) But something more than twelve million people were transported from Africa over the Atlantic in the period up to the end the nineteenth century. And it is certainly not the case that these twelve million were simply waiting on the coast and Europeans merely bought what was on offer—though even had they done so there is perhaps very little 'merely' about it. Nwokeji claims that 'the transatlantic trade...marked a watershed in the development of slavery in West Africa'.[25] And Iliffe argues that the new export business 'interrupted western Africa's demographic growth for two centuries. The trade stimulated new forms of political and social organisation, wider use of slaves within the continent, and more brutal attitudes towards suffering. Sub-Saharan Africa already lagged technologically, but the Atlantic trade helped to accentuate its backwardness.'[26]

To stick with the image of stolen cars—the fact that some managers in a car factory cooperated in industrial scale theft of cars would generally not be thought to count heavily for the defence of those from outside the factory who operated the scheme. Nor would it seem to make a fundamental difference that theft had gone on before the outsiders got in on it. Africans sold Africans for sure and not only to Europeans. But Europeans, Britons amongst them, by their almost insatiable demands, stimulated a business in which they might have chosen not to participate.

'We Weren't the Worst'

The thought that everyone was in it together, but somehow Britain wasn't the worst offender, is a thought with a longish history. Back in the mid eighteenth century some in Britain liked to think of their budding empire as one based on trade in contrast to the Spanish empire built on conquest,[27] and in the late nineteenth century for sure, Britain's global hegemony was, at least in British eyes, associated with an expansion of civilization, liberty, and religion.

Be that all as it may, how any of this helps to excuse practices of enslavement is unclear. British slavery was somehow nicer than other sorts seems like an argument with very little promise. Of course, Britain wasn't in at the beginning of the trans-Atlantic trade—Portugal was first on the scene and over the whole period, including with Brazilian ships, the major trader in enslaved people, transporting more than 5.5 million souls. But the British, although late to the trade compared to Portugal, came in in second place and transported something more than 3.25 million. From the second half of the seventeenth and through the eighteenth centuries, Britain was the leading nation in a trade which enriched Bristol, Liverpool, and Glasgow in particular, and was regarded as the foundation of Britain's naval prowess. By comparison French (1.3 million), Dutch (550,000), Spanish/Uruguay (1 million), and Danish (100,000) shipping, were much less significant. Perhaps surprisingly to some expectations, ships from the USA carried approximately only 10% of the British numbers (305,000).[28]

Numbers are often said to speak for themselves, but Britain's part in one of the major forced movements of people deserves at least a little more reflection and context. In 1750 the population of England, Scotland, and Wales is estimated at about 7.5 million.[29] The first British census of 1801, revealed a population of 10.5 million. So taking nine million as the likely population at the very height of the slave trade, we can say that Britain shipped a body of labourers amounting to more than 36% of its own numbers—which would be more than twenty-four million as a proportion of our present population.

So perhaps we weren't the worst, but we certainly did our bit—and 'someone did more kidnapping than me' doesn't seem an especially compelling plea in defence.

'What about the Vikings—or the Barbary Pirates?'

It is rare, I find, to discuss these matters without the Vikings or the Barbary pirates getting a name check. The Vikings, notwithstanding the rugged and romantic image they have acquired in modern filmography, were not averse to pillaging and enslaving—though to be fair to the Vikings, slavery (like pillaging) was a common feature of northern European life between the sixth to the late twelfth century.[30] The Barbary pirates have more of an image problem. The term 'Barbary pirates' is something of a catch-all for Islamic raiding out of the north African coast—but however they are identified, the scale of their operations was considerable, affected not just the Mediterranean, and caused terror to coastal settlements over many centuries. As late as 1631, the Irish village of

Baltimore suffered an attack carried out by Algerians (though led by a Dutch captain) in which something more than 100 people were carried off to slavery, some to staff the notorious galleys.

Now the problem with the Vikings and the Barbary pirates is just that they have no very obvious successors—let's leave to one side, for now, the other difficulty, that of identifying the descendants of their victims. The point is that it is going to be distinctly tricky to hold either Vikings or Barbary pirates to account any time soon.

But why are Vikings and Barbary called in evidence at this point? The objector's thought seems to be that since the Vikings and the Barbary pirates will get off scot free, it is tough that Britain should face a reckoning. Of course there can only be a modern-day reckoning for historic events where a people, nation, or society can be identified as in some sense the successors of those who did the harm in question—and more especially perhaps, are plausibly the recipients of the benefits which may have been accrued from the wrong doing. But it is hard to see that because that condition is only occasionally realized—and not realized in the case of the Vikings and Barbary pirates—that one should call off the whole business of reparations. Masses of fraud doubtless goes undetected, day by day, week by week, and year by year, and because undetected, unpunished—and some of the fraud that escapes detection may be a good deal more fraudulent than that which does get punished. Any fraudster's contention that he or she was, relatively speaking, unlucky to be caught, and that bigger, badder fish got away, might deserve just a tiny dash of sympathy. It is far from clear, however, that it is a reason for abandoning the case.

'Rather than Banging on about Reparations We Should Be Celebrating Britain's Leading Role in the Abolition of the Slave Trade and Slavery'

The 2007 commemoration of the bi-centenary of Britain's abolition of the slave trade in the British Empire followed this maxim and rather quickly turned into an opportunity for national self-congratulation. The celebration was thus informed by the sort of history described by Eric Williams when he observed that 'British historians wrote almost as if Britain had introduced Negro slavery solely for the satisfaction of abolishing it.'[31] Indeed when this sort of history gets into its stride, the story of Britain becomes a rousing tale of a freedom-loving land of liberty and enlightenment, with an important sideline in bringing civilization to more benighted countries and continents. Uninformed about any darker aspects of the story, British children growing up on this narrative may end up with an even rosier view than the one Williams found in those historians—with the idea perhaps that Britain abolished something it did not even practice.

The slightly more sober notion that Britain was at least out in the lead in the abolition of the slave trade and then of slavery, is—although indeed more sober—still somewhat misleading. The facts are slightly otherwise, and in truth Britain was rather late to the table when it came to freeing slaves.

Britain abolished the trade in 1807 and began the abolition of slavery itself with the Abolition of Slavery Act in 1833 ('beginning' because the Act envisaged a long period of 'apprenticeship' prior to full emancipation, so that some date emancipation to 1838 when the system of apprenticeship was abandoned). And yet from as early as the mid 1770s, the northern states in the American colonies, soon to become the constituents of the newly established United States, had either abolished slavery outright or committed to its gradual abolition—and by 1817 all had so committed. The French Revolutionary Government abolished slavery in 1794 (even if Napoleon changed his mind on that). A slave revolt in Haiti brought an end to slavery in 1804. Denmark–Norway abolished the trade in 1792. And Spain abolished slavery including in its colonies in 1811 (though Cuba did not comply). So we weren't first off the blocks—even if we weren't quite as tardy as the Pope who condemned slavery only in 1888 (when it was already done for, even in Brazil).

More to the point, there is a danger that the self-congratulatory 'we abolished slavery' line not only occludes, but actually seems to wholly discount, the agency of the enslaved themselves in gaining their freedom.

One side of this lies in the contribution made by the formerly enslaved in witnessing to the horrors of enslavement. Ignatius Sancho, who died in 1780, was a one-time slave who established himself as a man of letters and whose correspondence with Laurence Sterne gained him and the abolitionist cause considerable publicity. Olaudah Equiano is, however, perhaps the most celebrated author in a genre of literature which would be central to the abolitionist campaigns. He published his *Interesting Narrative of the Life of Olaudah Equiano* in 1789, and it went through many editions. But Ukawsaw Gronniosaw had been published in 1772 and Mary Prince would be published in 1831. The intellectual contribution of enslaved Africans was thus crucial from the very beginning through to the very end of abolitionist campaigning.

The other key element in the agency of the enslaved in accomplishing their emancipation lies in their consistent resistance to their captivity. The uncertainty and instability created by this determined resistance was a major factor in persuading even slave-holders that slavery might just come to an end with or without abolition.

There were revolts from the very beginning of the development of the sugar plantations. In the last quarter of the seventeenth century Barbados seems to have faced almost annual revolts—such that even the governor, who had the French and Spanish to worry about, described 'our black slaves' as 'our most dangerous enemy'.[32] The governors and councils of every island seem to have been constantly concerned by the huge discrepancy in numbers between British settlers and their enslaved populations—and individual plantation owners were equally aware of the disproportion in numbers between rulers and ruled within their own domains and lived in a fear of revolts which inspired their notorious brutality. The brutality did not, however, wholly deter unrest and, just to take the last two decades leading up to emancipation, there were major and large-scale revolts in Barbados in 1816, in Demerara in 1823 and in Jamaica in 1831–1832.

But resistance was equally a constant at a lower level of intensity. Open or subtle non-compliance with orders, sabotage, downing tools, feigning illness, and even refusing to eat, were just some of ways in which an oppressed workforce registered their opposition to the plantation regime. The white plantocracy, massively outnumbered by those they alleged were mere chattels, lived in fear of these chattels as of none others that they owned.

The successful revolt in Haiti was perhaps the most important element in sharpening the perception of risks to which owners were exposed by the varied but consistent noncompliance of their enslaved workers. So it was that abolition and compensation was highly acceptable to many of 'the interest', just because the prospect of losing everything to a successful rebellion seemed far from unlikely. 'The dangers of convulsions are greater from Freedom withheld than from Freedom granted to the Slaves' observed a report from a Parliamentary Select Committee of 1831–32.[33]

That pragmatic slave-holders may have favoured abolition serves to underline a wider point which the 'let's just celebrate the abolition' line overlooks. The reasons why the two abolitions finally occurred are complex. Eric Williams, in his iconoclastic *Capitalism and Slavery*, countered the favoured British story that abolition of the slave trade was a triumph of morality, with a vigorous defence of the thesis that abolition occurred because it served economic interests emerging in Britain's early industrialization.[34] Even if later historians have considered some of Williams' claims to be too strong, there is no doubt that many interests had to align before the abolitionist case could succeed. And amongst those interests was self interest, and in particular a perceived economic self interest in abolition—Adam Smith, in particular, advanced the argument that slavery was by its nature inefficient, and belonged to a bygone age. For a host of reasons, public opinion turned against slavery, but it is certainly not the case that the nation had turned from slavery as one, all spurred and only spurred by moral revulsion. Even thirty years after abolition in the British colonies, Confederate slave-grown cotton was still a staple of the booming industrial heartlands of Manchester and round about.

Schopenhauer found a pure and simple act of compassion in the payment of £20 million by the 'magnanimous British nation...to purchase the freedom of the negro slaves in its colonies'.[35] Given his resolutely gloomy disposition, it is surprising that Schopenhauer favoured this most favourable of interpretations. There is no reason, however, to go to the other extreme, and see wholly unadulterated self-interest in each and every abolitionist triumph, but somewhere between these two poles the moderately grubby truth lies.

But put this all to one side. Suppose we had been first at abolition, and suppose that abolition had been accomplished for only the very purest of motives. Even then one has to think that a simple celebration of abolition is somewhat dubious, although every abolitionist success in Parliament seems to have been greeted with solemn pronouncements on the glory of the moment. We can, of course, be glad that the abolitionists did indeed succeed (albeit with woeful compromises to achieve what they did)—but it seems difficult to argue that someone should celebrate the fact that they finally stopped doing something wrong, or that on account of their stopping, they shouldn't be held accountable for it. Michael Taylor poses a rather sharp question: 'Should criminals ever celebrate the end of their own criminality?'[36]

*   *   *

The objections I have covered thus far are not, for the most part, worthy of extended discussion—but I now turn to three further and more weighty objections. The first objection—that reparations are somehow objectionable in principle in the case of grave wrongs, as being incommensurable with them—can only really come from the likely recipients of reparations. The other objection, that reparations punish the present generation for the sins of previous ones, is likely to be the complaint of those who are being called upon to make reparations. The third objection might just unite both sides, likely recipients and those who may be called on to settle up—this is the thought that reparations are backwards looking and serve to inscribe the very racial divide which is slavery's most obvious legacy. Taken together, the exploration of these three objections allows for a clarification of notions which often occur in these discussions—of guilt, shame, blame, and responsibility—and a recognition of the limits of what moral repair can achieve.

'Reparations Are Objectionable in Principle—at Least in Cases of Very Grave Wrong—Since They Are Not and Cannot Be Commensurable with the Wrong Which Has Been Done'

If you damage my car in a drink/driving incident, you could apologize and offer me a sum to make it right. But suppose I lose my sight, or am left in a wheelchair or worse. In cases of such grave harm, there is no sum that will make it right. And in such circumstances the very offer of money might be said to trivialize the suffering of the victim. In more serious cases of grave injustice we might even go so far as to suggest that any payments dishonour those victims, and that any mere monetary payment should be dismissed as amounting to blood money.

That reparations would amount to blood money was a heartfelt complaint made by one side in the battle which took place in Israel as to whether the fledgling state should accept reparations from Germany after World War II. Perhaps the most outspoken proponent of this view was Menachem Begin—his opposition reaching its high point in the key and highly charged Knesset debate held on 7 January 1952. Begin declared: '16 million Germans voted for Hitler.... In the German army there were 12 million soldiers, millions in the Gestapo, the SA and the SS. From a Jewish stand point there is not one German who is not a Nazi, and there is not one German who is not a murderer. And you are going to obtain money from them?'[37]

Any discussion of reparations between Germany and Israeli, so soon after the Holocaust, was bound to be fraught—but what was inherently likely was rendered just about certain by the German's referring to their proposals as the 'Wiedergutmachung' programme. The term may be translated as 'redress', 'compensation', or 'reparations'—and even these words may have been problematic in the context. But the literal translation of the compound German noun, is 'making good again', a notion of what reparations might be in relation to the Holocaust which couldn't be anything but wholly inappropriate, not to say offensive. And pointedly the Israeli side in the negotiations always spoke of Shilumim, 'the payments'.

But it was the wider context, not just the terms used, which were bound to ensure that the proposal could not be received with a simple welcome. Whatever his own views may have been, Adenauer, the German Chancellor, could only advance the case for reparations in Germany itself on terms which were wholly unacceptable to the Israeli side. In Germany—where public opinion polls of the time suggested very little sense of any general responsibility for the Nazi war crimes, and very little sense that anything was owed to the Jews[38]—Adenauer prefaced the proposal for reparations with expressions of the innocence of the German people in general. (It was, in fact, as Susan Neiman documents in *Learning from the Germans*, characteristic of the first period of German recollection of the Second World War for Germans to think of *themselves* as the victims: 'For decades after the war ended, Germans were obsessed with the suffering they'd endured, not the suffering they had caused.'[39]) Furthermore, given the economic circumstances in Germany, Adenauer was bound to offer only a fraction of the estimated total of lost Jewish property which had been the basis of the original negotiations. Thus Begin and other opponents of the scheme could frame the proposed reparations as at once paltry, as offered on the false terms of 'making good again', and as unaccompanied by any real contrition.

The moral of this story, however, seems to me to be that an offer of reparations can be ill-framed—in particular where any proposed monetary settlement is not accompanied by obvious and explicit contrition, nor by the clear acknowledgment that money could never simply make things right where crimes against humanity are in the frame. Without contrition, and conceived as washing away wrong doing, reparations may well appear like an attempted pay off—blood money—and one that was quite simply offensive in the case of the suffering of the Jewish people. There is, in other words, every reason for those who have endured wrongdoing to challenge ill-conceived and inadequate programmes of recompense—and of course, if they see fit, to repudiate any offer made. But the fact that an offer of reparations can be ill conceived, is not an argument against the very making of an offer. It is rather a reminder that an offer of reparations needs to be made modestly and sensitively.

That reparations, in certain cases, cannot wipe the slate clean does not mean, however, that reparations will or should be refused. David Ben Gurion, the Prime Minister of Israel, advocated for the acceptance of the payments from German, and yet clearly accepted the point about the limits of reparation in the debate in which Menachem Begin spoke so powerfully on the other side: 'A crime of such magnitude [as those of the Holocaust] cannot be forgiven by means of any material compensation. Any compensation whatsoever, great as it may be, cannot be commensurate with the loss of life or forgive the suffering and anguish of men, women, children, the elderly and infants.'[40] And Frederick Douglass, in the last year of his life (1894), declared that 'for these terrible wrongs [of slavery] there is, in truth, no redress and no adequate compensation. The enslaved and battered millions have come, suffered, died and gone with all their moral and physical wounds into Eternity. To them no recompense can be made. If the American people could put a school house in every valley, a church on every hill top in the South and supply them with a teacher and a preacher respectively and welcome the descendants of the former slaves to all the moral and intellectual benefits of the one or the other...such a sacrifice would not compensate their children for the terrible wrong done to their fathers and mothers.'[41] But, as Darity and Mullen observe, Douglass did not conclude that no recompense should be offered or accepted, just because no recompense could ever constitute a full and final reckoning.

'Intergenerational Reparations Amount to "Visiting the Sins of the Fathers on the Sons"'

The previous objection to reparations comes from possible recipients. From those who may have to pay reparations for slavery and similar abuses the most common objection is that it punishes the wrong people. We have quoted already the doughty Mr Drax who insists that 'no one can be held responsible for what happened many hundreds of years ago'. Those who take this line often come on all biblical at this point and cite Ezekiel 18,20, which certainly has quite a ring to it: 'A son will not bear the iniquity of his father, and a father will not bear the iniquity of his son.'

No one should be held responsible or punished for what happened hundreds of years ago. I agree. But listen up. The case for reparations is not about anyone being punished or even being made to take responsibility for what happened. But that being said, Mr Drax (and Britain) should relinquish the wrongful gains of slavery and he (and we) are not being punished nor being made responsible for what happened long ago when we are asked to do so. Reparations are quite simply owed by someone who comes into the possession of wealth wrongfully obtained. It is the simple matter of possessing what cannot properly be deemed ours which grounds the case for reparations even if we had no part in the original wrong. This is very explicitly not a matter of visiting the sins of the fathers on the sons. We attach no blame or responsibility to the present generation when we say that they are bound to make restitution to those whose goods they currently possess—blame would only attach if, once the claim has been made, they decline to do what they should and hand over the funds.

What weighs with those who stress the 'not visiting the sins' line is just that there is clearly no sense in which the present generation committed, could have consented to, or even prevented, the deeds for which they might be asked to pay reparations. And there, in that sentence, are three degrees of participation that we would typically look for in attributing blame to someone, or in expecting someone to confess to feeling guilty in relation to certain wrongs.

Reliance on proverbial wisdom about not visiting the sins of the father on the son simply misfires here, however, since moral repair, and the reparations moral repair may require, are exactly not a matter of visiting the sins or guilt of the fathers on the children. The point is that reparations are not to be thought of as necessarily belonging on the side of retributive justice, but on the side of restorative or restitutionary justice.

The easiest way to mark this is simply to make the distinction in law between criminal and civil actions in relation to stolen property. A person who has stolen a bike would be expected to return the bike or equivalent and at the same time to face a charge of theft. The person who has received the bike in good faith, whether buying it from the thief, or inheriting it as part of an estate, would also be expected to return the bike or equivalent to the rightful owner (or that person's heirs). The rightful owner plainly does not lose title because the bike was stolen or conveyed by the thief. But equally the innocent recipient of the stolen bike would not be charged with theft. There is no question, then, of *punishing* the person who has received stolen property in good faith, and returning the stolen goods is exactly not a matter of punishment. And a museum is neither being punished nor blamed for something which happened more than a century ago when it is asked to return looted treasures to their original owners.

In many cases of reparations then, and obviously so in the intergenerational cases, no one's sins are being visited on anyone. There may have been sin or guilt at the origins of it all, but more to point here and now is the bare fact that someone has something which might be said to belong to someone else. This state of affairs needs to be put right. But the putting right is just that, and not a matter of punishment, however unwelcome this moral repair may be to the person who has to return what they thought of as theirs. And if this is the proper way of conceiving of reparations in the case we are thinking about, it is simply as the recipients or beneficiaries of wealth which rightly belongs elsewhere that we owe reparations—not as being responsible in any straightforward way for the misappropriation which slavery encompassed and for which our forefathers were to blame. Words from an insightful and important discussion of the issue as it arises for the United States of America cover as well the case of the UK: 'Our national inheritance was in considerable part unjustly acquired at the expense of African Americans, and, as a result, it is now unfairly distributed in respect to them. The issue here is not whether individual citizens' ancestors owned slaves, or whether they have personally benefited from discrimination against blacks, but that they now share in and benefit from an unjustly acquired and unfairly distributed national inheritance. *This is not a matter of collective guilt but of collective responsibility; and reparation is not a matter of collective punishment but of collective liability.*'[42]

'Okay—Maybe Some Money Is Owed by Way of Reparations. But Demands for Reparations Often Include a Demand for an Apology—and Since We Are Not Responsible for the Sins, We Can't Be Sorry and We Can't Apologise'

I have wanted to stress that the case for reparations, understood narrowly as a claim for monetary or other compensation, stands on the simple point that we unjustly possess what rightly belongs to others—and in a case dealing with the return of a stolen bike, or whatever, there would be no expectation that the present possessor of the bike (supposing them wholly innocent of any intention to deprive the rightful owner), should say sorry or apologize or express regret. All that would be required is that they return the bike.

Mr Drax and the United Kingdom, so I have suggested, should also return wrongful gains. But I now want to make an extra point. Even though no one is to be punished or held responsible for the original wrong of enslavement when reparations are admitted to be owed, in this case maybe the payer of reparations should feel ashamed and express regret or make an apology. Maybe as well as paying up, the morally sensitive Briton (at least, those for whom British history is their history, so to say), would need to own that original wrongdoing in a certain way, such that not to feel ashamed of it would be morally flat-footed or tone deaf.

Now words here are tricky, and what can or can't, or should or shouldn't, be felt or said, and by whom, are matters on which there may well be disagreement or uncertainty. But what seems clear is that however uncertainly we may tread in finding the right words—a struggle we are familiar with in framing almost any apology or expression of regret—it is from the cluster of words including 'sorry', 'regretful', 'remorseful', 'apologetic', 'ashamed' that we need to be drawing.

What we need to think about in the first place then, is what it is to 'own' our history. To say simply 'we are not responsible' for enslavement, even if we admit that we should pay up, risks missing an important element of the situation. That is to say that even if, in the case under consideration between Britain and the

Caribbean, the sins of the fathers *ought not to be* visited on the sons, the sons and daughters should arguably still, in a certain sense, own the sins of the fathers.

This cannot be a matter of owning the sins in the simple sense of saying that they are the present generation's own sins since, as we have said, they are not. But, contrary wise, modern-day Britons ought to own the wrong of slavery in a way that the recipient of the bike, five down the line from the original theft, need not, and indeed cannot. The person fifth in the chain of the bike's possessors and who is obliged to return it, is not expected to feel guilt or shame in regard to the original theft. The only feeling we might expect them to have is annoyance at finding that what they reasonably regarded as theirs is not. But we, I suggest, should feel differently about the iniquities of slavery and colonialism.

Just note, before we go any further, that 'we' is a difficult word here, given the make-up of modern Britain. The personal and family histories of many current inhabitants of the UK, some of whom arrived in the last fifty years, cannot be traced back through the story of British involvement in the slave trade and its aftermath. We may need to consider whether simply in virtue of making Britain your home British history belongs to you too—even if you arrived quite recently. But to avoid any such niceties, let the word 'we' here refer to anyone, like myself, whose family history (as far as I know) tracks back through the generations to Britons of the eighteenth or nineteenth centuries.

The notion that we—for whom this is our history—'should' feel something is a little ambiguous. It could seem as though I am laying down the law or making some proposals regarding proper moral sensibilities. (To those acquainted with moral philosophy, it might sound as though I am operating in a Kantian mode, and offering what he might have termed an analytic of guilt, shame, and responsibility: that is, an account of what we should properly think and feel.) But I don't mean to do that at all—rather, I mean (in the manner of David Hume) to describe and explicate the ways we usually seem to think about guilt, shame, and responsibility, and to reflect on what this means for the matter in hand. In Hume's terms, I am making some observations belonging to the natural history of our sensibilities.

Now Hume—since I have mentioned him—proves a useful guide here, as he was particularly interested in the judgements we make on ourselves, such as when we experience pride. Pride is a feeling of satisfaction in the self and people are proud of a host of things ranging from their mastery of a difficult language, to their new car, or even to their good looks. But there are lots of things of which one simply cannot be proud. As Hume puts it: 'A beautiful fish in the ocean, an animal in a desart, and indeed any thing that neither belongs, nor is related to us, has no manner of influence on our vanity, whatever extraordinary qualities it may be endow'd with, and whatever degree of surprize and admiration it may naturally occasion. It must be in some way associated with us in order to touch our pride. Its idea must hang, in a manner, upon that of ourselves; and the transition from one to the other must be easy and natural.'[43] To put it another way, it would be very odd for me to claim to be proud of a clown fish in the Pacific, or of an oryx in Arabia. For us to take pride in some object, occurrence or attribute, we must have some 'particular relation' to it, such that it is somehow 'associated' or connected with us. There must be some sense, in short, in which it is mine.

But what goes for pride seems to go for negative self-appraisals too—for shame and guilt for example. To take pride in something is to suppose that, on account of it, I gain prestige, worth, and standing; conversely to feel shame regarding something is, in certain cases at least, to think that it somehow detracts from that prestige or standing. And these negative appraisals, like the positive ones, are appraisals of the self, so just as there needs to be some connection between me and the something of which I am proud, so too here. You probably couldn't make much sense of my saying I feel ashamed of, let's say, Russian atrocities in the Ukraine, since these are not 'mine' in any way you (or I) could fathom.

Feeling ashamed of the behaviour of eighteenth-century British slavers and plantation owners seems a good deal easier, however—and is surely the flip side of a pride which seems very natural to very many people. Stick with pride for the moment: it is considered generally unremarkable that many of us claim to be proud of various connections to a variety of things of which we are in no sense the authors. People often express pride in their family name and history, in their university, in the profession to which they belong, or in their country and its history. In some way or another they may, of course, have contributed to the lustre of the group or institution of which they are proud, but that is by no means essential. To be proud to be British, for example, it is enough that you are British and Britain is yours, and to feel a sense of satisfaction in being connected to a nation which has (at least from time to time) valued its (own) liberties, produced Shakespeare, has a National Health Service (just), and (sometimes) opposed tyranny (at home if not abroad).

The irony here, of course, is that the very people who are most ready to dismiss current shame for past colonial wrongs as 'woke', are the very people who most loudly trumpet the glories of British history. Be that as it may—if it makes sense to be proud of that which I count as mine in some way even if I am most certainly not its author (my family, my university, my profession, my country and its history), then it surely makes just as much sense to feel ashamed of that which is no less mine and which I likewise did not cause. To be proud of Britain's abolition of slavery, but not to be ashamed of the fact of our conducting a slave trade for some two hundred years, suggests an entirely dubious pick and mix attitude towards what counts as mine.

What the exact scope of the 'my' and 'mine' is here, the scope which would account for our regular judgements, is not easy to say—except perhaps, that it is a wooden and unimaginative moral sense which confines the 'my' and 'mine' to the narrow bounds of actions I did or could have prevented. Of course, I cannot be ashamed of the practice of slavery in the way a British plantation owner in seventeenth-century Barbados could have been ashamed of it. Nor may I be ashamed of it in the way a descendant of a plantation owner might be expected to be. It is not my history in the sense it is hers. But it is British history, and on that account I can be ashamed, since it is what I think of as my nation and my people which perpetrated this crime. I might also be ashamed as a Christian, since it was a Christian continent which inaugurated and perpetuated a four hundred year trade in kidnapped peoples across the Atlantic. I may even claim to be ashamed simply as a human being, since humanity itself may seem disgraced and shamed by such inhumanity. So contrary to the simple thought that if I did not do it I can't be ashamed of it, shame seems to have a wider field of action.

Karl Jaspers, who struggled with the matter of German guilt in lectures given in 1945 in the raw shock of Germany's defeat, struggled in particular to find a way to articulate the responsibilities of individuals while also holding onto the more general responsibilities which might belong to others than the immediate perpetrators. Of perhaps the most general responsibility of all, which he termed 'metaphysical guilt', he wrote: 'There exists a solidarity among men as human beings that makes each co-responsible for every wrong and every injustice in the world, especially for crimes committed in his presence or with his knowledge.'[44] The 'especially' is right—but the first clause, in all its breadth, is right too.

This discussion has taken us beyond the bounds of restitution and recompense. Recompense for the crimes of slavery and colonialism are owed because we are beneficiaries of wrongs which still cause harm to identifiable others. That principle holds whether or not we are ashamed. But we should, I believe, feel ashamed of the original wrong—a wrong which we did not ourselves commit, of course, but which we surely amplify by disowning it, in particular by denying our duty to put it right.

Can we, or should we, then apologize for slavery? Let's go back to the thought I mentioned in passing back at the beginning of thinking about this objection, that in the context of the everyday apologies of everyday life, we are all familiar with the struggle of finding just the right words for saying sorry.

This can be hard enough where we are the perpetrators. 'I regret sleeping with one of your bridesmaids', said by groom to bride, misses the right note. 'Regret!' we can hear being shouted back. The gravity of the offence calls for words which mark that very gravity, and 'regret' may not, on its own, get it quite right.

Finding the right words may be harder still when we are not the perpetrators of the wrong. Parents regularly find ways of apologizing for their children, and children may sometimes, with less ease, find ways of apologizing for their parents or other forebears.

But sometimes apologizing can feel false even to a person who genuinely and in good faith is profoundly sorry for some past wrong.

Two things seem to me to be clear in the case of grave and historic wrongs such as enslavement. First, however uncertainly we may tread in finding the right words, it is from the cluster of words including 'sorry', 'regret', 'remorse', 'apologetic', 'ashamed' that we will surely need to be drawing. The second point is just that sorries are rarely constructed by individuals all by themselves. Apologies and expressions of regret are very often crafted by both sides. I may very well need to hear what you need me to say before I know what to say or how to say it. Moral repair is a process, not something which takes place in an instant in time, and for all the difficulties in framing an apology for enslavement, there is no reason to despair of the process of finding the right words in this particular instance.

'Reparations for Slavery Are Backward Looking, Encourage Claimants to Identify as Victims, and Risk Reinforcing the Very Racial Divisions Which Are at the Root of Past Injustices'

I have added this objection to the list of those which I regularly encounter in discussions of this topic, but I have to admit that the complaint my summary envisages is not the stuff of popular diatribe. Whereas the 'what about the Barbary pirates' line will often come in a pithy email which also questions my academic credentials and/or sanity, the objection I try to capture in this last numbered point is not so common. It may however be different in the

USA—according to Thomas McCarthy, 'A line of criticism of reparations politics frequently encountered among African Americans is that it is a form of racialized identity politics that reinforces rather than reduces the essentialism at the heart of modern racism and that promotes a sense of victimization that is culturally and politically debilitating.'[45] Now there are certainly differences between the case for paying reparations within the USA and the case for the payment of reparations from one nation to another, such as by the UK to the Caribbean—but however that may be, the objection that McCarthy expresses is surely relevant to both.

The objection's most general form is just that reparations are backward looking. By contrast international aid is concerned only with the neediness of the recipients—their misfortune needn't be anyone's fault in particular yet they still deserve help. Moreover, well-conceived aid might not only ignore the past, but look beyond any present acute crisis towards securing a better future. So, in its most general form, the objection says that it's better to focus on building that future, than to rake over the sorry past.

Humanitarian crises don't seem to be going away any time soon. And the call they make on our active compassion is undeniable. International aid has a major claim on our resources—and maybe thought of in rather different terms from reparations. Reparations have to do with an entitlement, whereas aid has to do with need, and these may not be regarded as morally equivalent. But I think it would be a mistake to see aid and reparations as necessarily in competition.

Resources are finite, of course, and what we attribute to one cause we cannot attribute to another. But while that point may be true in theory, in practice it misleads, since it is hardly as if the budgets of the wealthy nations of the world are such that there is some fixed pot of money for which aid and reparations must compete. The fact is that we could surely meet both claims, to a certain degree, if we so chose.

There is, however, a slightly deeper point here, which is that playing off the claims of the future against the claims of the past ignores the coherence of these claims, particularly in the case of the Caribbean post enslavement and colonialism. Present inequities—and the humanitarian crises which those inequities may precipitate—are in actual fact very often grounded in past wrongs. To cite an example we have used before, the challenges which climate change poses for the Caribbean result directly from the industrialization of the West. This industrialization, partly funded from the exploitation of the colonies as sugar plantations (and through other colonial ventures), has left the benefits of industrialization chiefly in our hands, whereas many of the most extreme harms of industrialization fall to those who knew nothing of those benefits. 'We should be concerned about the future, not the past' has a rhetorical appeal, but in the case we are dealing with it lacks force because addressing the past is very much a way of addressing the future too.[46]

McCarthy refers to a more substantial objection, which does not simply appeal to the supposed claims of the future over the past, but contends that reparations, in effect, perpetuate that past in the future. The case between the UK and the Caribbean differs from the case between African-Americans and others of the citizens of the USA—but in both cases, reparations would typically pass from a group predominantly racialized as white to one predominantly racialized as black or coloured. In any case, however the details may vary, any such transaction, so the objection goes,

96

reinscribes the very racial divide which lies at the heart of the inequities that reparations seek to address. In addition, reparations may risk exacerbating a sense of victimhood which discourages the enterprise and endeavour which would help overcome those inequities.

There can be no doubt that any programme of reparations cannot help but recognize, and thus potentially re-inforce, racial divides and associated mentalities. McCarthy, however, has a robust answer: 'it makes little historical sense to maintain that a group identification forged during centuries of brutal oppression could or should be dissolved while the injuries still persist. To proscribe race consciousness for remedial purposes without removing the racial inequities produced through racial classification for purposes of domination would be a fateful political error.'[47]

I take McCarthy's point to be that the attempted dissolution of race consciousness—however that might be achieved—whilst it would obviously attack the supposed reality of racial categories, may do nothing to dissolve the very real unfairness which race politics has produced. These deep inequities, of which disparity in income and wealth are the most obvious, would remain firmly in place even with the abolition of the polarities that fostered it. Perhaps these manifold inequities can and should be addressed through a politics of class, for example. And it is certainly the case that a racialized politics has threatened class solidarities, which might otherwise have been fostered between those racialized as black and as white.[48] But to replace race consciousness prior to dealing with the inequities would be an error, since it is from that place of inequity that Caribbeans, or African Americans, would compete in the imagined non-racialized world.

Race is a myth and a harmful one. We can only hope it is a myth we can overcome. But here and now race is not going anywhere— nor are the legacies of racism's great crime, enslavement. While we may need finally to overcome race to achieve a better future, any immediate occlusion or obscuring of race risks dissolving a classification while leaving behind that classification's woeful consequences.

Again, however, there is a danger of something of a false dichotomy here, as if a programme of reparations entails our simply tolerating racialization for the sake of trying to deal with its consequences. It need not be so. A programme of reparations (as we shall see in a later chapter) is not a matter of a simple transfer of cash—even if cash is what gets talked about because it seems to be such a sticking point for very many. On the contrary the moral repair we have envisaged encompasses an acknowledgment of the wrongs of the past, including in that the wrong of racism. Reparations are not due in place of a critique of racism; a critique of racism is likely a vital part of any serious programme of reparations.

This perhaps brings us finally to an aspect of this objection we have not yet mentioned—namely the suggestion that the seeking of reparations encourages victimhood as a prime mode of self-identification, when such a self-identification is socially, economically, and culturally debilitating.

I find something deeply troubling in this objection, alongside finding it mistaken. The mistake, I think, is just that the claim for reparations—exactly as opposed to any claim for aid—comes from a place of confidence and strength. Against the gross wrongs that were inflicted on their forebears, a people stands up and claims its rights. And it claims them exactly as an entitlement. Yes, that people may have been victims of discrimination and all that has flowed from it. But their claim arises from an assertion of their true and proper standing, not from a dwelling on their mistreatment.

To call this objection troubling is to see it from another angle—as choosing to cast the potential claimants in the role of victims when such a role denies the historical and moral accomplishments of the African diaspora. The point is this—that although race is a science fiction, it is manifestly a cultural reality. Racist thought has imposed itself on our thinking such that it has provided categories we routinely deploy to identify ourselves and others. And yet the appropriation of racist thought by those transported across the Atlantic and their descendants has not been uncritical. The racist devaluation of certain racial types, intended to create, instil, and propagate shame and self-loathing, has been resisted and overcome to such an extent that the disvalued characteristic has become a symbol of pride and resilience—the writings of Marcus Garvey and of the later négritude movement stand out as an early, self-conscious, and explicit rejection of the racist judgement on blackness and the transformation of that negative judgement into a positive celebration. Thus an identity which was inflicted as a form of othering has been taken up and transformed into a powerful and proud self-identity, which has been central to vast cultural achievement, of which the modelling of moral resistance within the black churches has been just one vital element.[49] As James Baldwin says, the story of his people is of those who 'in the teeth of the most terrifying odds, achieved an unassailable and monumental dignity'.[50]

It would be very curious, would it not, if after centuries in which those from whom reparations may be due have profited from the mistreatment of the enslaved and their descendants, those same people were now to worry that to address this mistreatment in a serious and substantial way risks fostering 'victimhood'? On the contrary, a programme of reparations would provide an acknowledgment of the false terms on which the relationships between those racialized as black and those racialized as white have been conducted. And it would be premised on a powerful and compelling demand for justice, not charity, from those who have been wronged.

From this high plane, however, we need to come down. So much for the objections to reparations in principle. For some who accept the case for reparations in principle, it is practical issues—**who** gives **what** to **whom**—which sinks the whole thing in a welter of concerns about fairness, feasibility, and cost. So it is to these practical questions that we must now turn.

5

From Principle to Practice

Who *Should Pay* What *to* Whom?

The history of the relationship between the UK and the Caribbean is a history of wrongs, and we should try to make amends for it. There are some well-rehearsed objections to the very idea of making reparations, but on examination they don't seem compelling. That's the story so far.

It is, however, easy to imagine that someone, with us to this point, now hesitates. Reparations may seem a good idea in principle, such a person may concede, but the practical issues, however—**who** gives **what** to **whom**—are considerable; indeed research on public attitudes suggests that addressing these practical issues is, reasonably enough, crucial to support for reparations.[1]

It is the **what**—or more precisely—the **how much**—which is likely the real sticking point. If money is part of a package of reparations, questions are bound to arise as to how the right sum can be calculated. And supposing such a sum is plausibly identified: if it is considerable, as the scale of the wrongs in question rather suggests it will need to be, is it affordable? But it is not just the **what/how much** that may be the subject of controversy. **Who** will bear the cost? And **to whom** should any payments be made?

It is all very well to support the case in principle, but is there a plausible and workable proposal which would take us from theory to practice?

What

As a matter of fact there is a substantial proposal on the table, put forward by the Caricom Reparations Commission. Caricom (short for the Caribbean Community) is a grouping of fifteen member states and five associated members, representing the interests of countries across the region. In 2013 Caricom established a Reparations Commission with a mandate to 'establish the moral, ethical and legal case for the payment of reparations by the government of all the former colonial powers and the relevant institutions of those countries, to the nations and people of the Caribbean community for the crimes against humanity of native genocide, the transatlantic slave trade and a racialized system of chattel slavery.'[2] In March of 2014, the Caribbean heads of government endorsed a *Ten Point Action Plan for Reparatory Justice*, addressed not only to the UK, but also to Denmark, France, Sweden, Portugal, and the Netherlands—that is, addressed to the major actors in the slave trade and in colonization of the Caribbean.[3] The plan is comprehensive and asks for:

1. A full formal apology for the wrongs of slavery and the subsequent treatment of emancipated peoples.
2. The right to repatriation for descendants of enslaved Africans who may wish to seek to return to Africa.

3. An indigenous peoples' development programme, to advance the well-being of the descendants of the original inhabitants of the West Indies, who were decimated by western diseases at first encounter, and have suffered discrimination and poverty ever since.

4. The establishment of cultural institutions in the Caribbean to tell the stories of the enslaved from their side.

5. Support in addressing the public health crisis in the Caribbean, arising from the extraordinarily high incidences of chronic diseases (such as hypertension and type II diabetes), related to deprivation and ill-treatment over many generations.

6. Assistance in the eradication of illiteracy since 'At the end of the European colonial period in most parts of the Caribbean, the British in particular, left the black and indigenous communities in a general state of illiteracy. Some 70 percent of blacks in British colonies were functionally illiterate in the 1960s when nation states began to appear. Jamaica, the largest such community, was home to the largest number of such citizens.' Such high levels of illiteracy represented a significant drag on social and economic development.

7. An African knowledge programme aimed at connecting people of African descent with their roots.

8. Psychological rehabilitation aimed at 'healing and repair of African descendants' populations'.

9. Technology transfer to enhance access to science and technology:

For 400 years the trade and production policies of Europe could be summed up in the British slogan: 'not a nail is to be made in the colonies'. The Caribbean was denied participation in Europe's industrialization process, and was confined to the role of producer and exporter of raw materials. This system was designed to extract maximum value from the region and to enable maximum wealth accumulation in Europe. The effectiveness of this policy meant that the Caribbean entered its nation building phase as a technologically and scientifically ill equipped backward space within the postmodern world economy. Generations of Caribbean youth, as a consequence, have been denied membership and access to the science and technology culture that is the world's youth patrimony.

10. Debt cancellation to address the problems faced by governments seeking to overcome the inheritance of slavery and colonialism:

Caribbean governments that emerged from slavery and colonialism have inherited the massive crisis of community poverty and institutional unpreparedness for development. These governments still daily engage in the business of cleaning up the colonial mess in order to prepare for development.

The pressure of development has driven governments to carry the burden of public employment and social policies designed to confront colonial legacies. This process has resulted in states accumulating unsustainable levels of public debt that now constitute their fiscal entrapment.

This debt cycle properly belongs to the imperial governments who have made no sustained attempt to deal with debilitating colonial legacies. Support for the payment of domestic debt and cancellation of international debt are necessary reparatory actions.

It might be said that the most remarkable thing about the CRC's comprehensive proposals are just that they have been made at all. As Walker points out, it can never be taken for granted that a wronged party will seek reparations in the wider sense of moral repair: 'Those who have suffered serious harm or grave injustice may struggle to summon the trust and renew the hope that repair requires, and they may yet have good reasons to withhold these.'⁴ The CRC's invitation is significant exactly in looking to repair relationships with former colonial powers who have thus far done little to indicate their willingness to engage with such a project or process—or rather, have generally signalled their disdain for the very idea of reparations.

In aiming at moral repair, the CRC's proposal is not and could not be a simple demand for monetary compensation. A simple payment of money may, of course, be termed reparations—as in the case of the payments from Germany to Israel after the war. And in some rather special circumstances, monetary payment may be thought sufficient to restore and repair a broken relationship—though not in the case of Germany and Israel, of course. Money may be a wholly adequate currency for righting wrongs which are wholly monetary in nature. But even where the harms which have been done are broader and deeper, money may serve to address certain aspects of the case, while doing little or nothing in relation to non-material harms.

The Commission is not making a simple demand for monetary compensation—it is a much more considered and comprehensive proposal for a range of measures to deal with the long-standing and deep-seated wounds which enslavement and colonization inflicted on the region. And it begins where moral repair is bound to begin, with the need for acknowledgment and apology. And yet—so the practically minded objector will surely notice—each of the ten points in the plan for reparations, barring the apology, would need funding. None of these proposals is costed, however, it might also be pointed out. So while an objector might concede that all the suggested actions are worthwhile in themselves, we need to get a handle not just on what would improve the situation of those who have been disadvantaged or harmed, but on what could be deemed to be owed by those who committed or caused the wrongs, or, more to the point, by their descendants who are still beneficiaries of the wrongs done. CRC has not named a sum of money—but the question as to what funds are owed naturally comes to the fore.

There is, I think, something rather special about the practice of enslavement which actually demands that money be part of almost any plausible scheme of moral repair. There could be cases where money would have no obvious place in addressing historic wrongdoing. Imagine a particular ethnic or religious group within a nation has been subject to various constraints and prohibitions which have curtailed their freedom of speech, for example, without necessarily curtailing their ability to engage in business and make a living. Such was perhaps the position of dissenters from the established church in early-nineteenth-century England for example. Suppose a contemporary case for recognition of and apology for a wrong such as this—money may have no part to play in the moral repair of such a situation.

There is something about reparations for enslavement, however, which seems inevitably to raise a question about cold hard cash. Why? Well a few pages back I posed a question as to who gives *what* to whom—and as I have said, and as the CRC proposals envisage, reparations need not be only material or monetary but may involve expressions of apology or regret, the return of cultural artefacts, the construction of memorials or the institution of memorial occasions, the extension of rights of residence, and countless other possible gestures, actions, or initiatives. But where reparations for slavery are in question, the issue of money arises with a particular logic and force: for all its other wrongs (and they are many), the essence of slavery, and of the bonded labour which followed it, is just that these were means of appropriating, or expropriating, the value of a worker's labour. The appropriation in enslavement of something for which in modern economies most people are paid a wage means that the loss of money, whilst not the worst of enslavement, goes to the essence of what it was. Thus money seems likely to be essential to any scheme of reparations in relation to slavery.

In the United States a good deal of work has been done in trying to conceptualize and represent the material and other losses suffered by the enslaved, and to consider how, by, and to whom reparations should be made. W.A. Darity and K.A. Mullen's recent book *From Here to Equality: Reparations for Black Americans in the Twenty-First Century* is both an authoritative treatment of the history and an important contribution to further discussion. And in this discussion, money is certainly central.

An early post-Civil War proposal for reparations, which was never implemented, would have given land to the newly emancipated: forty acres and a mule for each formerly enslaved family of four was the plan. Subsequently proposals for reparations have taken as their point of departure the value of this proposed grant of land, or alternatively the value of unpaid wages, or the purchase price of enslaved people. Such proposals have typically also tried to allow for inflation by representing historic values in terms of their contemporary purchasing power. In addition to allowing for inflation, however, these different sums may be compounded at different rates to capture the likely return on money invested over the last more than one hundred and fifty years.

Darity and Mullen find these approaches unsatisfactory, however, specifically in that in fixing reparations at the time of emancipation, they fail to 'reckon with the economic injustices...[and] social penalties blacks incurred after slavery and well into the twentieth century'.[5] This has led to an extraordinary disparity in levels of black and white income (a disparity which cannot be explained by class alone), but Darity and Mullen attach more significance to differences in wealth than to difference in income. As they see it, 'the racial wealth gap' is 'the most robust indicator of the cumulative economic effects of white supremacy in the United States', and they regard 'wealth, or net worth, as a more powerful measure of economic well-being than income'.[6] For a host of reasons, so they argue, it is wealth, not income which counts in terms of life chances.

Their calculations of the sum needed to address the wealth gap arrive at a huge number. The figures from 2016 show that the differences in mean household wealth by race was approximately $795,000.[7] 'Multiplying $795,000 by the U.S. Census Bureau's estimate of about 10 million black households yields an estimate of a total reparations bill of $7.95 trillion'[8]—which, just to be clear is $7,950,000,000,000, or, in UK terms, £6,600 billion ($7,950 billion).

In relation to the case of Britain and the Caribbean which concerns us, Darity and Mullen's approach is problematic. While in their context the gap between black and white wealth arguably provides the best marker of the disadvantages African Americans have experienced, there is no such obvious marker indicative of the disadvantages suffered by the inhabitants of the Caribbean.

It is true enough, as we have said, that economic injustice no more ended at emancipation in the Caribbean than it did in the United States. But we have no obvious proxy for the white American family as indicating where the average Caribbean family would now be financially without the history they have suffered—and thus no obvious route in estimating the extent of the loss which this history of injustice may have entailed.

Other aspects of their proposals are important, and we will return to them. But in trying to capture and express the economic injustice of enslavement in the Caribbean, as against the case in the USA, we have one bit of hard financial data which seems worth reckoning with, even whilst recognizing that relying on it does not allow us to encompass the entirety of that injustice. That piece of data is the actual sum of money set aside and paid out as compensation at the time of abolition.

Parliament designated £20 million as recompense, not to the enslaved of course, but to their purported owners, for the loss of what the enslavers deemed, and what Parliament in effect conceded, was their property. The most obvious thing to say about this sum of money is just that it ended up in the wrong pockets, as many leading abolitionists said at the time. But beyond that, there is a reason for pausing on this number and examining it. The key point is that in broad terms the compensation which was conceived as covering the loss of labour suffered by the enslavers can, with some plausibility, be reconceived as representing the loss of the value of labour suffered by the enslaved. Or as it might be put: 'the price of a slave summarizes the capitalized value of the economic exploitation inherent in the slave system'.[9]

It is all but certain that abolition would not have occurred without the payment of compensation to the purported slave owners.

Notwithstanding the widespread distaste for slavery which the abolitionist campaigns elicited and marshalled, enslavers adroitly positioned themselves in relation to abolition as simply potentially wronged property owners. With an appeal to the sanctity of private property, enslavers were able to draw many allies to the cause of compensation who were otherwise indifferent or even opposed to the continuation of enslavement. As Kathleen Butler puts it: 'even the abolitionists defended the principle of compensation'. 'The social and political events of the early nineteenth century forced the government to recognize that most of the middle class would interpret uncompensated abolition as a direct attack on the rights of private property.' The 'upheavals and riots' which were a feature of these years had 'threatened the property of the gentry and factory owners alike', and 'newly elected Whig representatives of the industrial areas of the Midlands and the North proved to be as susceptible to the [West Indian] Interest's appeal to property as the conservative Tory gentry'.[10]

While the principle that compensation would have to be paid came to be a presupposition of the abolitionist case, the principles according to which compensation would be calculated were more contested. The government's opening bid proposed to turn the slaves into unpaid apprentices for a period of twelve years and offered a loan of £15 million to the planters—the apprenticeship scheme allowed the enslavers to retain three-quarters of the slave's labour and the loan was conceived as making up the difference. In the parliamentary debates which ensued, the abolitionists objected to the proposed twelve years apprenticeship as too long and the enslavers objected to the loan—they estimated the value of their alleged property in enslaved people at £47m, and the loan as wholly inadequate. The government gave on both points—the apprenticeship scheme was shortened to six years, and the loan was converted into a grant of £20m. At the next stage of the process, the £20 million was divided between the respective colonies based on the estimated value of a colony's slaves as a proportion of the total value of all slaves. In turn each colony valued its slaves as they fell into different categories, such as tradesmen, field labourer, children, and the aged.[11] So the amount of compensation paid for an enslaved worker varied from island to island, and from person to person.

The horse-trading that took the government's initial proposals to the statute book as an Act of Parliament, and then to a worked-out scheme that paid compensation to individual owners, was governed as much by pragmatism as by any clearly articulated and rigorously applied principles. Nonetheless, in broad terms, the amount paid to the purported owners, together with the period of apprenticeship, was aimed at recompensing them for the prospective loss of the labour of their enslaved workforce. It is possible, however, to treat the sums here involved as representing not the prospective loss to the enslavers, but alternatively as representing the retrospective loss of the value of their labour which had been suffered by the enslaved.

The sum that was actually paid in relation to the enslaved people in the major plantation islands was £16,356,668[12]—it is worth giving the precise sum just to indicate how very careful was the calculation of the amount due to the purported slave-holders. Now £16,356,668 in 1838 (the date of the report on the awards made under the Abolition Act), amounts to £1.9 billion at present values according to the Bank of England Calculator. Doubtless other ways of expressing the current value of historic sums would give other amounts, but the more important point to note is that that original sum, if invested wisely, would not simply have held its own against inflation, but would have accrued in value. There would have been a return on this sum—and year by year, a return on the return. To represent the value of £16.35 million now, cannot then be a matter of merely translating that sum's purchasing power in the 1830s into a current day value. Rather that original sum must be compounded at whatever is deemed a plausible rate of return. Naturally there is debate to be had about what that rate should be— Darity and Mullen take 4%, 5%, and 6% as plausible candidates for representing the combined rate of return and rate of inflation. To take a conservative approach for the moment, let's compound the initial sum at 4%. £16,356,668 invested at 4% for 188 years from 1834 gives us £29,770,662,889—near enough £30 billion.

But that isn't the half of it, as they say. For even if we reckon that this, with its various assumptions, is an interesting figure, it can't be what we are looking for, for a very important reason. (We pass over for the moment the fact that we have thus far ignored the value to the owners of the period of apprenticeship, which was a part of the compensation package, even if it was not paid in cold hard cash.) The point is that all we have done so far is consider whether that £16 million may represent the loss of the value of their labour to the single generation of those who were emancipated by the 1833 Act, as that £16 million would have accrued in value for their descendants had it been invested. But how are we account for the losses to previous generations of enslaved people, let alone—and I propose indeed to let alone—the losses to the subsequent folk who lived as bonded labourers, and who, even after that, suffered from profound disadvantage and lack of opportunity in colonial and post-colonial societies?

As for the enslaved people prior to that final generation, we can do a calculation along the following lines. At emancipation there were 655,780 enslaved people in the main British Caribbean islands—so the compensation of £16,356,668, however distributed in detail, averaged out at £24.94 for each person. Now the total number of Africans forcibly transported to the Caribbean is said to be around 2.3 million. If we imagine all those people as being alive at the time of the payment of compensation, all of them unremunerated for their labour, we can arrive at a value for that unremunerated labour in 1834—that is, 2.3 million multiplied by £24.94, giving a total sum of £57,362,000. In terms of present-day value that amounts to £5,679,244,735. But, as we have said, it is the value of the sum invested which is perhaps most significant— and this sum compounded for 188 years at 4%, gives us not £30 billion which is the compound value of the actual sum paid out, but £105 billion.

The point of these calculations is not to arrive at a figure which claims to represent precisely the losses sustained by the enslaved. The point is a much more modest one, which is simply to take one part of the compensation for lost labour paid to the enslavers, and imagine what that sum would look like had it been paid to the enslaved and some of their forebears. What is important to bear in mind, however, is that however large a number £105 billion may seem, it is almost certainly too small to serve as a proper representation even of the value of the labour which was appropriated on the plantations, let alone for the wider 'costs' of enslavements. We need to note the following points:

1. In the first place the apprenticeship scheme was also part of the compensation paid to the enslavers—or to put it another way, arguments would have been made by the West India interest for an increase in the £20 million that

was set aside had there been no such scheme. (The market value of the enslaved people at the time of emancipation was said to be closer to £50m, as slave owners were keen to point out.) So we would need to take this point on board to reach a better estimate of the value of the lost labour, and would then arrive at an even larger amount. Approximately 80% of the enslaved people for whom compensation was due were from the main plantation islands of the Caribbean; so taking the plantocracy's valuation of the enslaved seriously, they reckoned they were due approximately £40m for 655,780 people—that is approximately £60 per person. So, multiplying that by 2.3 million (the number transported to forced labour in the Caribbean), gives us £138 million. And if we compound that at 4% over 188 years we get the even more impressive figure of £251 billion.

2. In the second place, using 2.3 million as the number of people whose labour was unremunerated captures only those who were transported. It does not count the number of those who were born into enslavement in the Caribbean and lived and died before emancipation. (Just to be clear, plainly some of the 655,780 who were the subject of compensation payments after emancipation were Caribbean born—but the number I have used as a basis for the estimate of the value of lost labour uses *only* the number of those who were transported. I have not found it possible to find any reliable data on the number of those born into enslavement in the Caribbean during the period prior to emancipation; there are estimates for the USA.)

3. In the third place, as previously pointed out, emancipation did not bring freedom and justice at the drop of a hat;

instead, plantation owners across the Caribbean typically found ways of maintaining the labour force in new forms of servitude. The calculation of £105 billion makes no allowance for the years of economic exploitation after emancipation.

4. As I stressed at the outset, there is no attempt here to represent the even more grave non-monetary deprivations and sufferings of slavery.

5. We have compounded at a relatively conservative 4%.

With those caveats, we now have a possible bill for reparations. £105 billion is a low estimate based on the partial compensation represented by the cash payment to the owners of enslaved people. Adding in the value of apprenticeship as part of the total package of compensation gives us £250 billion. What should we make of these numbers?

There are different ways of looking at these sums—and whereas I have been stressing that this is an underestimate of what may be considered due, the first reaction to the estimate may be that it is very large indeed. There is no personal context, even for the world's leading billionaires, in which £105 to £250 billion is anything other than a dauntingly large sum of money. And even if we look at the figure as a debt per person or per household in the UK, it seems weighty—more than £1500/£3700 per person (105/250 billion divided between 67 million) or £3750/£8900 per household (105/250 billion divided by 28 million).

Arguably, however, the context of personal or household finance is not the right one in which to locate this figure—it needs to be seen in the more relevant frame of public expenditure and debt.

UK government spending varies year to year, but in round terms the UK government spends approximately £35 billion per annum on defence, £110 billion on education, £180 billion on health and £285 billion on what budget documents refer to as 'social protection'—meaning pensions, housing benefits, and other welfare payments. According to the Office for Budget Responsibility, the Government is expected to spend £1185 billion in the year 2022–2023, with a deficit against income of some £177 billion. That deficit is itself smaller than the £312.6 billion deficit in 2020–2021, when measures associated with COVID produced the highest deficit since the Second World War.

Even set besides these figures, £105–250 billion is not insignificant. But there again it is perhaps better to contextualize a one-off capital payment by reference to the national debt to which the usual yearly deficit on the national budget itself contributes. To cite the OBR again, they expect public sector net debt to stand at approximately £2.6 trillion (that is, two and half thousand billion) and to be increasing in cash terms over the next few years, even while decreasing as a percentage of national income. To give another way of looking at that figure for national debt, it represents £91,000 per household—which (to go back to our £105/£250 billion), is about 10.5 to 24 times the per household putative debt for reparations.

There is no way that the suggested bill for reparations can be regarded as a trivial sum—except perhaps when we go back to the original decision and look at the sum set aside for compensation in its very own context. According to the parliamentary reports of the day, the mention of £20 million produced laughter. Members of the House of Commons 'were shocked by their own extravagance'[13] when they passed this measure—as well they might have been. £20m in the 1830s represented 40% of the Treasury's annual income and 5% of GDP. 40% of the Government income today (£1000 billion) would be £400 billion, and 5% of UK GDP (about £20,000 billion), would be £1000 billion. Set against a sum which caused a certain giddy hilarity in the House of Commons, the putative bill of £105–£250 billion as recompense for just some of the depredations of slavery might be judged a relatively modest and sober number—especially when, according to 'the IMF…the combined GDPs of all of Britain's former colonies [in the Caribbean] amounted in 2018 to just £69 billion'.[14]

All these figures may cause any but an accountant's head to spin. So let's leave them aside for now. The real question is not whether the sum, looked at from whatever angle, is significant or insignificant, trivial or otherwise—the question is whether, if it is arguably due, it can reasonably be found. And here the question of **what** is to be paid becomes connected with the question as to **who** should do the paying. In the context of the UK's national budget and wider finances, £105–£250 billion is significant without being wholly daunting. Yet the question of how such money could be raised and from whom is a serious one.

Who

Thus far we have relied, perhaps implicitly, on the notion that it is the UK who should do the paying. But the blank attribution of responsibility to the UK, for all that it is a simple and straightforward answer, risks unfairness in at least two different respects.

The first point is that the UK is a vastly different country from the country which practised and abolished slavery and then went on to engage in worldwide colonialism. Specifically the make-up of its population is very different—the present day population is not simply the successors of those who were here in 1835. People have come and gone—particularly since the 1950s many people have settled in the UK, not only from former colonies. London in particular, but the UK as a whole, has a new population, not one simply comprised of descendants of the old one. The census of 2022 has some telling statistics: of the nearly 60 million residents of England and Wales in 2021, some 10 million—or 16.8%—were born overseas. The proportion of those born overseas in the smaller Scottish population (about 5.5 million) is itself smaller, but still around 10%.

Would it be fair to ask this new population to share in bearing the costs of reparations for what went on long before they arrived in the UK? The question is all the more pointed if, as is the case, not only some recent migrants, but many from a previous generation, are themselves the descendants of the enslaved populations to whom reparations may be thought due. It seems to add to the difficulty to notice further that many recent immigrants to the UK may themselves be experiencing poverty.

The second point follows on rather naturally—and is that the existence of poverty within the UK poses a risk of another or added unfairness, depending on how the cost of paying reparations falls on the population of the UK. When my advocacy of reparations to the Caribbean was reported in a certain right-leaning London newspaper, an indignant reader wrote to me to complain that reparations would likely be paid by 'hardworking tax payers'. I was tempted to suggest that we might try to identify some lazy tax payers to bear the cost—even better, some lazy non-tax payers. But joking aside, the complaint latches onto an important point.

Wealth and poverty are relative terms, of course, both between and within nations. According to standard definitions of poverty used in the UK (that is, as having an income below 60% of the median), some 20% of the population is said to be experiencing poverty.[15] Of course by most metrics the average UK resident has a higher income than the average resident of the former colonies in the Caribbean. Yet it must also be noted that many of those in relative poverty in the UK are poor in a more absolute sense: surviving at or near a subsistence level, struggling to feed themselves for example, or unable to heat their homes. According to the Joseph Rowntree Report *UK Poverty 2023*, '2.4 million people, including 550,000 children, experienced destitution' in 2019—where destitution 'means going without the essentials we all need to eat, stay warm and dry, and keep clean'.[16]

Now with such levels of hardship within the UK, anything that might add to the burdens of the poor hardly commends itself as just or equitable. The risk is exactly that in addressing one injustice we may exacerbate another.

These two points raise legitimate concerns about the fairness of the UK population as an undifferentiated whole footing the bill for reparations. They do not sink the case for reparations, however, but rather strongly point to the need to ensure that the cost of reparations must somehow be borne more equitably.

At this point Darity and Mullen's distinction between income and wealth becomes relevant. Their argument is that it is disparities in wealth, rather than disparities in income, which are the real markers of continuing injustice, and that it is disparities in wealth that need to be addressed in framing reparations for African Americans. I want to look at that from the other side—from the side of the question as to who may have to pay reparations—and suggest that these same disparities suggest where the cost should fall.

Wealth and poverty are intergenerationally sticky, within countries and between them. It is because wealth is sticky between the generations and between countries that we in the UK still benefit from the wealth that accrued from slavery. Money is exactly not like bubbles, gone in a moment—rather it hangs around, as does the lack of it. But as that point is true between the UK and the Caribbean, it is also true within the UK itself. Wealth is passed and preserved between the generations—and Piketty's *Capital in the Twenty-First Century* has drawn attention to the fact that inequities in distribution seem to be increasing, not diminishing, in the contemporary world.[17] To put it in crude terms, the nations and families who were enriched by slavery have typically passed that wealth within their nations and down their family lines; those who were impoverished by enslavement or, at least, did not accrue much of a share in the wealth they created have often been stuck with their poverty. These facts suggest that we need to seek justice not only by paying reparations, but by finding a way of paying them fairly—and that means specifically that the cost of paying them should certainly not fall on the poor.

What is the answer? It so happens that there is a very recent report entitled 'A Wealth Tax for the UK' from the Wealth Tax Commission—having nothing to do with reparations of course—which argues that there is merit in a one-off (rather than an annual) wealth tax.[18] Such a tax would, according to its advocates, 'raise significant revenue in a fair and efficient way, be very difficult to avoid, and would work in practice without excessive administrative cost'.[19] Depending on various assumptions, and choices, it could be expected to raise as much as £260 billion—and to do so in such a way, of course, as not to burden the poorest sector of the populations. Coincidentally, that £260 billion exceeds by a small margin the higher number of the two we have calculated as a possible bill for reparations.

This proposal raises many further issues—but it is not my intention to review those, nor to consider in any detail other ways in which the UK may choose to settle a claim for reparations. All I want to do is to point out that there is, on the table, a scheme for raising funds which may address our responsibility for the poverty of the West Indies, whilst also being sensitive to the inequities of modern-day Britain.

Of course, a wealth tax may fall on some of the descendants of the enslaved, or some very recent immigrants to the UK who have no links through the generations to the colonial period. The answer to this, however, is surely that those who have achieved economic success in the UK, wherever they started and however they have done so, have themselves benefited from the country's social, institutional, and cultural capital. This capital was immeasurably enhanced by the wealth generated by colonial slavery. There is no injustice then, in asking the newly wealthy, even if themselves recent migrants to this country, to contribute to the bill for reparations through a tax which is blind to details of origins.

To Whom

Lastly and more briefly there is the 'to whom' question. To whom precisely should reparations be paid?

I really have little to say here, other than that reparations of the kind in question here are a matter between sovereign nations, and that it would be for the recipients to determine how best to administer and distribute any reparations due to them. It would not be for those who might pay, to repeat a colonial posture and adjudicate those plans.

The point that is important, however, is that reparations would be paid not to individuals but to a nation, and that a nation has an existence over generations. Ideally reparations would be given or received in a form which would allow them to contribute to the range of projects envisaged by the Caricom Reparations Commission; and the point of these projects is not to assist individuals directly but societies more generally. The suite of initiatives would address the traumas of the past but would aim to do so by building the capacity of the islands to create better futures.

One regular objection to reparations of any kind is just that the money may be poorly spent, whether received by individuals (which is not in question here) or by governments. There is a particular worry that the money may benefit elites and not the generality. It would seem to me that any such concerns, whether or not they are valid, could be finessed by CARICOM designing or designating an institution with an international charter or status, perhaps in association with the UN, to receive reparations from the UK or from other colonial and slaving nations. Such a body could be charged with distributing funds with a view to investing in education, health, and other projects which would aid the wellbeing, development, and growth of local communities and economies.

The population of the Caribbean is approximately 45 million, but the most populous countries in the region (Haiti, Cuba, Dominican Republic, and Puerto Rico) were not British possessions. In fact, the formerly British islands have a total population of barely 6 million—though often with a considerable diaspora.

£105–£250 billion might seem a large sum, at £17,500–£41,600 per head—but Norway, with slightly fewer people (and fewer development needs), has a sovereign wealth fund with holdings in excess of $1000 billion (£800 billion). Properly directed reparations on the scale we have conceived them could make a difference to the Caribbean—without, however, being anything like the embarrassment of riches which Britain and its plantation owners once enjoyed.

Conclusion

The very idea of reparations has a troubling ring in certain ears. The most immediate association of the word for many people will be with the reparations demanded by the victorious allies after World War I, the burden of which is generally reckoned to have weakened German democracy and have been a major factor in the rise of the Nazis. This is an unhappy precedent to be sure.

There is perhaps a more general feeling that any plan for reparations will be beset by practical issues. The purpose of this chapter has been to consider what funds might be considered due and thus available to underwrite the important proposal for reparations which has been made by Caricom. That sum has been set by reference to the original and very considerable amount paid to the slave owners. My argument has been that the estimate of what is due, which builds from that starting point, is probably as afford-able as was that original sum. Moreover there are ways of funding the payment of reparations which ensure that the money is not raised from those who can ill afford it and, furthermore, ways of ensuring that the money ends up working for the good of those who deserve it. None of this has been worked out in any detail, but there is enough to show, I suggest, that any supposed practical problems can very likely be overcome.

But someone might say: practical or impractical, this is fanciful stuff. No European government has given the slightest hint that it sympathizes with the payment of reparations. A plan for reparations is a lovely idea—but it is going nowhere.

Postscript

Sometime after this book was submitted for publication, and in the last stages of production, *the Brattle Report* appeared (more fully, *Report on Reparations for Transatlantic Chattel Slavery in the Americas and the Caribbean*).[20] The main body of the *Report* was produced by a team from the Brattle Group, an international consultancy which addresses complex economic questions especially around valuation for corporate and other clients. In this case the team from Brattle were responding to a brief provided by an Advisory Committee, chaired by the Honourable Patrick Robinson (a Judge of the International Court of Justice) and established through the University of the West Indies' Centre for Reparation Research.

The Brattle Report is undoubtedly a landmark in thinking about reparations just because it offers serious quantification of multiple harms experienced during enslavement and amongst the descendant populations of the formerly enslaved. In effect it importantly furthers the work begun by Caricom's Reparations Commission by providing specificity to the 'what' (or 'how much') of reparations.

The Report deserves more careful consideration than is possible in a postscript. The initial point of consideration, however, would most likely focus on the huge disparity between the sort of sum I have suggested as a starting point for discussions (£105–250 billion) and the headline figure proposed by the Report. Britain alone is said to owe $24 trillion dollars—that is $24,000 billion (approx. £19,000 billion).

It must be sufficient here to make two points.

The first is to say that the concern of my proposal has been to focus on the losses to the enslaved and benefits to the enslavers which arguably carry over on both sides into the present day. It is for the payment of reparations in regard to these particular losses, I would contend, that the argument is strongest. The misappropriation of labour was absolutely central to slavery and to its present day ramifications. The Brattle Report looks at a much wide range of damages, however, including for example, for the gender based violence of enslavement and also for the loss of liberty suffered by the enslaved. In these and other cases the estimates of damages are based on serious analysis, but there is a fundamental question which requires extended discussion regarding the proper scope of reparations which may be held to be due, ethically or legally. Gender based violence was one of the grave wrongs of slavery, as was the loss of liberty, but to compensate the present generation for the sufferings of others (and not for their own present deprivation resulting from slavery) raises further issues which I have not explored in this book.

The second point is merely to stress that my chief object in this chapter has been to overcome the often encountered objection that a proposal for reparations, however plausible in theory, founders in practice in arriving at a hard cold number. My point has been to claim not that the number I have ventured is **the** number for the amount due in reparations (even where reparations concern chiefly loss of the value of labour), just that it is a number which, for the reasons I have given, has a claim to be taken seriously in further discussions and negotiations. Any such further discussions and negotiations will certainly now need to engage seriously with the Brattle Report, and in particular with its analysis of foregone earnings. But the common perspective is just that the estimation of numbers here is a perfectly rational procedure which admits of debate and discussion.

6

'It Ain't Gonna Happen...'

I suspect we can all, at this point, hear a weary voice. It is the voice of people who like to think of themselves as realists, but whom others may describe as cynics. And what they say is simple: 'it ain't gonna happen'. The cynical realist—or realistic cynic—puts to one side the questions of principle discussed a few chapters ago, and may think it not worth bothering even with the matter of practicality, which we took up in the last chapter. The realist may simply wash his or her hands of the whole business with the hard-headed thought that, in the end, the payment of reparations is a matter of politics more than of principle and practicality. You can argue the principles all you like. You can answer each and every objection. You can even put a practical proposal on the table. But those alone, even all taken together, will not make it happen. Politics is politics, and politics is not about principles and arguments and ideals, nor even about those combined with mundane considerations of what is possible or feasible. Politics is about interests, or more specifically about self-interest. A fool and his money are said to be very soon parted; but a nation and its wealth, whether or not arguably ill-gotten, tend to stick together. The payment of reparations is little more than a pipe dream. So says the weary realist.

I confess that on a bad day I give way to no one when it comes to weary pessimism. That Britain should do the right thing in this matter seems highly unlikely. Tony Blair couldn't bring himself to apologize for enslavement. The possibility that a government will be ready not only to do that, but to hand over a substantial sum in reparations, is surely vanishingly small.

But there again.... In 1785 no one would have thought it likely that the slave trade would be abolished some thirty years later, and slavery within the British empire some twenty years after that. Adam Smith was an opponent of slavery, and yet he seems to have entertained no thought that its end was nigh. And remember, or—since most people seem not to know this—reckon with the fact that in 1785, 75% of the world's population was enslaved in some form or other. As Seymour Drescher has it, at the end of the eighteenth century, freedom, not slavery, was 'the peculiar condition'.[1]

Even if by the 1780s, as we have noted, the intellectual argument against slavery was widely accepted, its deep embeddedness in the economy of the nation argued for its likely continuation. George Hibbert, admittedly no disinterested bystander, and a man well able to look out for himself and other enslavers, may just have been being honest when to a Select Committee of the House of Commons in 1790 he 'confess[ed] that the abolition of the slave trade was a measure not in my contemplation as not believing it probable'.[2] As Porter puts it, 'widespread antipathy to slavery coexisted with a substantial interest in its continuation. In particular, Britain's involvement in the African-Atlantic slave trade, her commerce in tropical commodities from the West Indies, her capital investment in shipping, the plantation economies of her colonies, and the prospects for future growth in the West Indies, all continued to flourish'.[3] And yet notwithstanding these powerful material interests, the slave trade and slavery itself did indeed come to an end in many places in fairly short order. And in part this was due to the utopian, unrealistic, crazy, thinking of the abolitionists, against the 'it ain't gonna happen' of the realists of their day.

Now the 'in part' does a lot of work in that last sentence in the last paragraph—the end of slavery was 'in part' due to the efforts of the determined abolitionists. There is no reason to swallow the Hollywood version of the story of abolition which says that liberty came about as a result of the efforts of one or at most two good men—Wilberforce being one, Clarkson the other. There is every reason to think of the causality here as depending upon the lining up of a host of reasons and considerations, economic, political, diplomatic, and especially, of course, the wholly pragmatic appreciation of the determination of the enslaved to fight against their enslavement. The nature of the real world politics of abolition was not lost on the abolitionists of course—thus, to take just one example, they 'presented the ending of the trade as damaging to the French and part of wartime strategy'.[4] But none of this denies that active 'utopianism' played a part—by which I mean, not only dreaming of a radically different future than the present, but also acting for the sake of its realization. Moral critique, and the campaigning and popular agitation it inspired, certainly contributed to what seemed almost unimaginable to very many—the demise of the slave trade and of enslavement.

So as regards reparations, I don't buy 'it ain't gonna happen', though I will buy 'it ain't gonna happen tomorrow'. The case for reparations is compelling, I think, but many of the elements in the case are unfamiliar (a proper grasp of the history, for example), or misunderstood (that reparations have nothing to do with punishment, for instance), or are relatively newly made (that the payment of a significant sum is practical and affordable). More to the point, in the end reparations must be a matter between governments— but as yet none of the former European colonial powers has acknowledged the case for reparations in relation to their role in the trade in enslaved people, in their deployment of enslaved labour in their colonies, or for any exploitation of the unenslaved even after legal emancipation.

The case of Germany and Namibia may be thought to open a chink in Europe's solidly defensive posture—and in 2021, Germany's foreign minister, Heiko Maas, announced that German and Namibia had brokered a 'reconciliation agreement' relating especially to the atrocities committed in the early 1900s against those who were then known at the Herero. 'In the light of Germany's historic and moral responsibility', Maas declared, 'we will ask Namibia and the descendants of the victims for forgiveness.' This seemed like a major step forwards. But after the announcement, agreement seems to have unravelled, with Germany backing off from any use of the word 'reparations', and representatives of the descendants of the Herero expressing dissatisfaction with the framing of the payments and their amount.[5]

The unresolved situation between Germany and Namibia is not a ground for great hope, then, so much as an object lesson in just how tricky such sensitive discussions can prove to be. In any case, with or without this example, there is surely a long way to go in gaining acceptance for the case for reparations which, like the case for abolition back in 1785, has yet to gain significant recognition and popular support.

So the question arises as to how this case is to be advanced? Assuming it is not acceptable simply to sit on one's hands in the hope that tomorrow will arrive soonish, what can be done here and now to hasten the day?

Reparations with a Small r?

Margaret Urban Walker's important book on *Moral Repair* suggests that in cases such as the one we are considering, there can be a responsibility for actors below the level of nation states to step up. This is not in place of that higher responsibility, but rather to stir its acknowledgement. It is this responsibility or opportunity for lower level actors which I wish to explore here, notwithstanding scepticism towards it even from advocates of reparations, such as Darity and Mullen.

Walker notes that the work of moral repair in relation to a long-standing and deeply embedded wrong, such as that against African Americans in the United States, will very likely require governmental initiatives—but she also notes that 'the work of restoration almost certainly needs to be done in many different kinds of communities, groups and institutions. Locally responsive actors can prime larger communities for a truer appreciation of their responsibilities and consequent tasks.'[6]

Darity and Mullen, however, are critical of what they recognize as 'the growing movement for so-called reparations at the local and state levels or financed by individuals and private organizations'.[7] This movement is based on an insight such as Walker's, that within large-scale communities, perhaps especially national communities, smaller communities or groupings have a responsibility and opportunity for 'priming' the larger body. But Darity and Mullen discuss these efforts under the heading 'Missteps' and declare: 'Blatant opposition represents an obvious obstacle to black reparations. But there are more subtle obstacles, additional barriers created by presumed supporters of redress'[8]—and this movement for local reparation falls under this edict.

Their major concern is that efforts by state, local, or private actors could not hope to fund reparations to the amount they deem necessary. So, to take two examples—'Evanston, Illinois, which professes to have inaugurated the nation's first municipal reparations plan, would require about $3.85 billion to close, independently, the $350,000 per capita racial wealth gap. The city's annual budget is closer to $350 million.'[9] And California's 'reparations task force' faces a similar inability to fund what Darity and Mullen judge to be requisite: 'It is impossible for the task force to design a plan that will eliminate the racial wealth gap for eligible black Californians, about 2 million in number, since the cost would be $700 billion, more than double the state's current $260 billion annual budget.'[10] Their suggestion is that these lower level actors would be better spending their money lobbying national government, and that any 'local initiatives' should be described as "racial equity" projects rather "reparations"'.[11]

The terminological issue we might just set to one side for the moment. Certainly if 'reparations' are framed as the sort of sum which might be deemed proportionate to the harm which has been suffered by a community, actors at a lower level than the community which bears final responsibility will almost certainly offer much less than necessary. I'm tempted to distinguish Reparations from reparations. But the real question for us is not whether such below national level measures should or should not be termed reparations, even without the capital, but whether ahead of a government to government settlement, reparations by other bodies represent nothing more than a distraction.

There are two particular institutions or communities in the UK with which I am associated, both of which have begun to address their role in transatlantic chattel slavery. I want to describe what each has done and assess the merits of these initiatives in the context of a nonetheless clear commitment to final resolution of the issue as a matter for national government.

Enslavement, a Cambridge College, and the Church of England

Trinity College, Cambridge is one college in a university which has rather prided itself on its abolitionist credentials. Wilberforce and Clarkson were undergraduates at neighbouring St John's College, and it was under the premiership of Charles, Earl Grey, a Trinity alumnus, that abolition finally occurred. Wilberforce and Clarkson, in particular, are remembered around the university and its hometown in street names, for example, and both Wilberforce and Clarkson have achieved wider fame as the resolute heroes of the abolitionist tale.

If the university and colleges have readily celebrated these abolitionist connections, they have been less conscious of the very existence, let alone the depth, of their entanglements with practices of enslavement. Only now, more than two hundred years on, are they coming to terms with that history.

In 2019, when the issue of universities' historical links with practices of enslavement was being taken up especially in the United States, the Vice-Chancellor of Cambridge established a

'Legacies of Enslavement Working Group', which produced a report in late 2022.[12] Alongside this initiative, some of the individual colleges of the university took up the challenge to fill out their own particular histories of links to enslavement. College histories, written or oral, tended to overlook the existence of any connections with the institution of enslavement. Certainly in the case of my own college, Trinity, there was no public recognition of the fact of any links of any kind, when the truth is that the College's entanglements with the slave economy amount to a veritable thicket.

It would be easy enough to focus only on the headlines concerning some clear associations—especially since the headlines are quite eye-catching. A former Master of Trinity, Robert Smith (a very distinguished mathematician), made many gifts to his old College, including a legacy at his death in 1768 of South Sea stock, to the value of £2000 (£260,000 in present day values, according to the Bank of England inflation calculator—let's not complicate it by compounding it). This legacy was used to pay for a window depicting Isaac Newton in the College's Wren Library, and for the making or renewing of a rather fine common room. Isaac Newton was the College's poster boy well before his own death, and the renown of the intellectual star of the scientific revolution was also celebrated with a magnificent statue in the College chapel (funded by Smith, again, and said to have cost £3000, a little bit more than the legacy). All this information is in the public domain.[13] What is not in the public domain is that Smith's investment in the South Sea Company can be traced back to when it was the leading company trading in enslaved people from West Africa.[14] What is absolutely clear is that the man whom Smith sought to honour, Isaac Newton, had himself also invested in South Sea stock when the

South Sea Company was very definitely trading in enslaved people and was known to be doing so—though he seems to have made this investment after he had resigned his Fellowship and left Cambridge.

But to focus on headlines such as these—to focus, that is, on the direct benefits which may have come to the college from investments in the trade in enslaved people and on the star names connected with such investments—is to risk overlooking the depth and extent of the college's entanglements with the trade and its legacies. Particular instances of particular connections may be noteworthy; but what is more remarkable still is the generality of connections which effectively embraced the community viewed as a whole.

It is easy enough to be tempted again to look for direct connections at the end of Britain's involvement in enslavement, and to home in on the number of alumni who received some of the compensation dished out in the 1830s. And this certainly produces some startling results. The database of the Centre for the Study of the Legacies of British Slavery, at University College London, collates the records relating to that compensation, and in addition tracks the histories of plantations back into the eighteenth century. It records some 80 Trinity alumni as claimants on the register. But since the official records of the compensation payments are themselves a little sketchy, and because academic affiliations were no part of those records, that 80 is by no means the full number. And to date I have identified at least another 40 Trinity alumni who are associated with claims for compensations.

These 120 men claimed for more than 25,000 enslaved people, out of the total number of 655,780 for whom compensation was paid—that is more than 3.65% of the total, at a time when Trinity graduates represented something like 0.026% of the British population. In other words, the college is, in a manner of speaking, 150 times over-represented among the claimants. And some of the very biggest claimants are Trinity students—two Hibbert brothers received compensation for more than 3000 enslaved people, and William Hinds Prescod (a leading owner of plantations in Barbados) claimed for 1750.

But for all that these numbers are striking, the extent of the connections is much wider. Two things need to be noted.

First of all, by the 1690s and onwards a steady stream of West Indians, as they were termed, arrived at the college—that is, the sons of merchants, traders and planters resident in the Caribbean, whose wealth and social ambitions led them to seek the status and connections which a Cambridge education secured. Bear in mind that colleges were smaller then than now, and that Trinity College, although the biggest in the university, was perhaps admitting somewhere between only 14 and 35 students a year at the beginning of the eighteenth century, and only regularly just above 50 in the century's last decades. But of the approximately 3210 admissions in the century, perhaps 225 were West Indians—7% of the whole, and in any one year perhaps higher. Typically the West Indians were not admitted as regular students, but as Fellow Commoners, with special gowns to mark out their higher status, and with the privilege of eating with the Fellows at the so-called High Table. For this special treatment, they paid higher fees—proving again that there is really no such thing as a free lunch, or dinner, even at the High Table. These fees, by the way, were customarily paid in kind, in the form of silver objects such of candlesticks, cutlery, or more decorative items, some still in the College vaults to this day.

But it is the second point which really completes the picture. Of all the connections which undergraduates made at Cambridge, the most significant ones were probably those which led to marriage. Wealthy West Indians (or rather their sisters) made ideal partners for more regular undergraduates. Many of these undergraduates were the offspring of aristocratic and gentry families and, especially if they were not first born (and even sometimes if they were), they were very much in need of funds. Equally, the sisters of established families were desirable partners for the newly wealthy West Indians seeking to rise up in the world by gaining status through connection to English landed families. By such alliances the West Indians gained social capital and the English elite gained capital. These were marriages made in heaven, and they produced generations of undergraduates from slaving families, whose social ascent is as striking as their success in holding on to the wealth and privilege which enslavement had first bought them.

Take just one example. If Martin Madan of Nevis, an early slave owner who died in 1703, is regarded as the founder of the Madan fortunes, he could, if blessed with foresight, look down the years and see his sons, grandsons, great grandsons, and even great, great, great grandsons, studying at the college, achieving worldly success as Members of Parliament, bishops and the like, and connecting themselves by marriage with the children of aristocrats and other establishment families.

So great is this interweaving of the children of slaving families with Trinity's more regular students hailing from the gentry and above, that by the end of the eighteenth century and just prior to emancipation it is hard to find an alumnus who is not somehow connected with the slave economy, whether directly or more indirectly through family, business, or other ties. Even notable abolitionists find themselves in bed, so to speak, with slave-owning dynasties—thus the later Madans could claim distant kinship with certain Trinity members of the Gurney family, whose sympathies were generally abolitionist, and whose uncle, Samuel Gurney, had been one of Wilberforce's staunch allies. And the Gurneys were also linked with other major and early slaving families, such at the Eliotts, the Byams, and the Woodleys, all in turn with Trinity connections.

This interweaving of new and old wealth in a complex network of marriage and family is not only noteworthy in itself. It surely also goes some way to explain why abolition was so long in coming, and why, when it was achieved, it was on terms so very favourable to the slaving interest. This interest, although perhaps small if you count the heads of plantation owners, and of traders and merchants who were directly engaged in the sugar trade, was allied with a much more significant number of individuals and families through the bonds and ties of marriage and kinship. Indeed, in an age before impersonal banking, when trust was an essential element in the conduct of business, these ties were not merely incidental to the enterprise of transatlantic enslavement, but in fact constitutive of it. Or as Catherine Hall has tellingly put it, 'capital' in the eighteenth century 'was not anonymous—it had "blood" coursing through its veins'. 'Businesses were built on kin connections.'[15]

We have already said that emancipation did not bring freedom pure and simple, far from it. And in the subsequent history of the Caribbean, the college and its members played a role as significant as in the pre-emancipation period. Some Trinity plantation owners took the opportunity provided by compensation to divest themselves of West Indian interests, but others maintained their interest and managed to run plantations, even under 'freedom', on lines hardly different from the old ways. Other undergraduates continued to find opportunities in the colonies as administrators, lawyers, judges, statisticians, scientists, and clergy, supporting and sustaining the colonial enterprise. Meanwhile, back at home so to speak, Trinity academics (such as Sir Francis Galton, 'the father of eugenics'), contributed to the development of the spurious race science which became something like orthodoxy in the early twentieth century and would spread a baleful influence over social attitudes even down to today.

Provided with this outline understanding of the College's connections to enslavement and its legacies, the College agreed in early 2023 to three initial steps. No one used the word 'reparations', but the actions in question mirror the model of the three or fourfold action required for moral repair.

1. In the first place, the College agreed to appoint an established researcher to document and chart the College's links and ties with the history of enslavement. Much is already known. But a proper part of moral repair is a full understanding and acknowledgment of one's actions, and in particular of the harms they may have caused. The research project is aimed at that fuller and informed understanding and acknowledgment—and will need to include engagement with affected communities.

2. In the second place, it was agreed that the College's shameful connections with enslavement and the riches it brought, should be formally recalled and memorialized as a matter of sorrow. A formal way of doing that was found

by adding to the annual Commemoration service, when the College remembers its founder and benefactors. Now, at the opening of that ceremony, the College confesses its failure to bring to bear on the institution of enslavement the critical spirit which it celebrates in the achievements of its intellectual luminaries, including (most ironically of all) Isaac Newton. As is appropriate, wider discussions will be initiated to consider other fitting ways of remembering the injustice of enslavement and expressing regret at the College's links with it.

3. In the third place, the College agreed to contribute £1 million to the establishment of scholarships for students from the Caribbean, to be spent over five years. Again, this is a first step which is but a token of a commitment to address aspects of the continuing harms of enslavement. How that should properly be done by a college with Trinity's history, and with assets of somewhere in the region of £2 billion, is an outstanding question.

To go back to the distinction I proposed between Reparations and reparations, any effort by Trinity College, and by the many other universities and colleges in the UK who are beginning to address their histories (such as Glasgow and Bristol Universities, and All Souls' College, Oxford, for example), can only be tokens of what is really due—reparations if you like, not Reparations. They do not acquit the nation of its own higher responsibility. But let's allow that for the minute and leave it there while we look more briefly at another example of another institution beginning to come to terms with its history. We shall need to ask presently whether these efforts are a help or a hindrance to the bigger cause.

The entanglements of the Church of England with transatlantic slavery are quite as extensive as those of Trinity College, and perhaps even more striking. The Society for the Propagation of the Gospel owned a plantation in the Caribbean and had its enslaved workers branded with the word 'Society'. The typical claimant for compensation after emancipation was an Anglican Tory, a support of the status quo in religion and in politics—and very many, indeed, were ministers of the Church. And ministers of the Church of England in the Caribbean were much more likely tolerant of racial hierarchies and harsh labour conditions than critical of them—in contrast, for example, to Baptist ministers, who in the nineteenth century played a significant role in working especially with the newly emancipated in their struggle for political and labour rights. Even after emancipation, one Anglican clerical luminary of the emerging and deeply conservative Oxford movement, William Hurrell Froude, would write from Barbados to another, John Henry Newman, denouncing the abolitionists and their cause in ranting and racist terms.[16]

There is a very full and sorry history to document here. The Church of England seems to have begun its reckoning elsewhere, however—with a Report on the more direct, or perhaps more readily quantifiable, matter of the origins of some of its current assets.[17]

Many of those assets are held and managed by the Church Commissioners, which back at the beginning of the nineteenth century absorbed an earlier fund known as the Queen Anne's Bounty. That fund, at its early inception, had invested in the South Sea Company, which was a (possibly *the*) leading European company trading in enslaved people in the years 1714–1739, during which time this was its chief and widely publicized activity.

According to a recent Church report, 'Over the course of at least 96 transatlantic voyages during this period, the South Sea Company purchased and transported human beings as chattel property; 34,000 enslaved people in crowded, unsanitary, unsafe, and inhumane conditions. It also transported enslaved people from Caribbean islands to Spanish-held ports in mainland America. Investors in the South Sea Company would have known that it was trading in enslaved people.'[18] When the South Sea Company ended its involvement in the trade in 1739, 'Queen Anne's Bounty had accumulated investments in South Sea Company Annuities with a value of around £204,000...which may be equivalent to about £443 million in today's terms.'[19] And even in the years after the South Sea Company ceased to be connected to the trade, the Church's investments and holdings in the company continued to yield an income for Queen Anne's Bounty.

The recent report entitled *Church Commissioners' Research into Historic Links to Transatlantic Chattel Slavery* documents these early investments and other benefactions which may have come to Church funds from those connected with enslavement up to and just after emancipation—a gift from Edward Colston of Bristol being the outstanding example. All in all, this is a thorough report, based on extensive and careful research, resulting in a clear and authoritative account of at least some of the most direct and important financial ties linking the Church of England to the transatlantic trade. This clear account is accompanied by an explicit expression of regret, and, to add the third element, by action aimed at moral repair: 'Nothing we do, hundreds of years later', says the Report, 'will give the enslaved people back their lives. But we can and will recognise and acknowledge the horror and shame of the Church's role in historic transatlantic chattel slavery and, through our response, seek to begin to address the injustices caused as a result.'[20]

Specifically, on the last point, the Church Commissioners have committed £100 million, to be expended over a nine-year period, to support a programme of relevant investment, research and engagement. The investment will be directed to communities affected by historic slavery, the research will be aimed to widen knowledge and understanding of the historic links to enslavement, and the engagement will focus on using the Commissioners' voice as investors to address and combat modern slavery. The entire programme will be overseen by a newly formed group with membership from communities impacted by these historic wrongs.

In the context of this book, the examples I have just discussed serve as illustrations of how thoroughly entangled many institutions were with the whole business of enslavement, even when this was very specifically not their business as such. But in this chapter these accounts of the actions of two bodies in addressing their connections with the practices of enslavement serve a more immediate purpose: as giving us a basis for assessing Darity and Mullen's scepticism regarding sub-national or local programmes of moral repair or reparations. My suggestion is that contrary to their suspicion, institutions and communities below the national level may have an important role in, to use Walker's term, 'priming' higher, and specifically, government agency.

Most importantly, the actions of institutions may serve to model to government what is required of them. The recent report from the Church Commissioners could only ever be part of the Church's response to its past, and there is much more to be said about Christianity's complicity with, and complacency regarding,

the development of the transatlantic slave trade and the exploitation of Africans in the Caribbean. But if, for example, the Church
of England committed to doing on a larger scale what it has begun
with its enquiry into its direct linkages with enslavement via
investments, this would be a powerful statement in the context
of national thinking and discussion.

To complete the task it has begun, the Church of England would
itself need to do three things.

First, it would need to sponsor the conduct of a full and detailed
report into its complicity with enslavement. It would need to appoint
a distinguished commission to produce an authoritative statement
covering not just the Church's general acceptance of the practice
of enslavement, but its actual engagement with it—the fact, for
example, that the Church of England, as owner of the Codrington
Estate in Barbados, was a recipient of compensation for the loss of
the enslaved, who had, even while held by Christians, been beaten,
branded, bought, and sold right up to the time of emancipation. In
producing such a report, the Church would model the truth telling
and acknowledgement from which moral repair begins.

As a result of these findings, transparently shared, the Church
would need further to make a clear and formal apology for the
wrongs which any report would document. Perhaps this apology
would be the culmination of a national day or period of mourning, repentance, and shame which this history surely deserves.
And perhaps a national day of mourning should be an annual
occasion—maybe in the course of Lent—such is the stain of this
history on the life of the Church. Other and better ideas might be
forthcoming. The important point is that the history that detailed
research will document will demand not just to be admitted, but
to be admitted in a spirit of sorrow.

And then, in the third place, as a token of its remorse, the Church would need to devote resources, including very probably money, to addressing some of the many harms which are the continuing legacy of the sorry practice of enslavement. The question of how to make reparations, understood here specifically as concrete actions aimed at making amends, requires thought and consultation—it is certainly not a matter of paying to make it all alright, nor even is it only about money. The institution of an annual commemoration of the history of this injustice may itself be a part of the reparations which are due, so too physical memorials, and so also a commitment to ensuring that teaching on the sin of racism is central to Church's ministry of education. What is requisite is a combination of words and deeds, which together seek to address the disadvantages and harms that still afflict the heirs of the enslaved. In whatever form reparations may take, the Church should be ready to use its resources to begin to make amends in a significant and costly way.

Acting thus, the Church of England might grasp the opportunity which its rather peculiar standing and status and wealth offers—to witness to the nation as a whole what it might be for the nation itself to remember the wrongs and injuries of the past and to begin to move beyond that past, and indeed to move beyond a present which still bears those scars.

Of course, this action could not by itself acquit the nation of its greater responsibilities, nor would the resources which the Church might commit come near the sort of sums which might finally be judged appropriate. Yet such is the place of the Church of England in national consciousness, that its action would challenge the state to do the right thing, engage its own members in discussion and debate, and demonstrate, though admittedly at a lower level, the coherence and feasibility of moral repair.

The case for action by Trinity College—or other actors—is analogous. Within the context of public discussion and debate, an academic institution possesses a different authority from that of a church. A church may typically claim and be recognized as having a certain moral authority; a university would hope to possess an authority as an arbiter of historical and scientific truths. Thus colleges and universities, in virtue of their commitment to research and knowledge, may be thought to have a particular responsibility to document their own intellectual failings and to contribute to contemporary public understanding.

Darity and Mullen, while recognizing that the task of persuading a majority of the American population that reparations are due to African Americans is a daunting one, nonetheless find some room for optimism in recent modest shifts in public sentiment. A survey in 2000, so they report, found that 59% of African Americans favoured 'monetary compensation to African Americans whose ancestors were slaves', but only 4% of those racialized as white favoured such compensation. A survey conducted just over 20 years later, in 2021 showed a shift: the numbers now stood at 86% of African Americans and close to 30% of white Americans, with support amongst those under 55 even higher.[21]

The dynamics of public sentiment and its formation are surely complex and difficult to fathom. But in contributing to the development of public support for reparations, the actions of many institutions have a part to play. Without wishing to comment on the US case, which has its own particularities, I would contend that action by universities and colleges (including my own), and by the Church of England, have merit in and of themselves and can be regarded as advancing the case for reparations rather than hampering it. Of course, the sums involved in any institutional commitments are small in relation to what may be deemed appropriate, but they are something and they achieve some good for present-day individuals even whilst proper recompense remains outstanding. And the sort of projects a college or university may facilitate can be highly generative, just in the sense that education, research collaborations, and capacity building projects are impactful investments which reach out beyond the immediate beneficiaries. There can be no suggestion that scholarships for Masterships programmes, or funding for medical training on the scale that small actors can fund, will in any sense come near providing what is necessary, but they do provide some relief and benefit and demonstrate on a small scale what can be achieved.

But there is a further point, well brought out by McCarthy in his insightful essay on reparations which I have had cause to cite previously. Those who believe, as I do, that the case for reparations is compelling, and yet who also believe that there may as yet be no clear public support for reparations, will likely further believe that a public conversation or debate—even if stimulated by churches, universities, or other institutions—is exactly what is needed to create the understanding to ensure that the national debate finally occurs. McCarthy is writing about the USA but I believe his conclusion applies to the UK:

> the reparations movement could ignite a public debate in our mass-mediated public sphere and…this could eventually prove to be of great 'public-pedagogical' significance in raising and reforming public historical consciousness. The structured forums provided by public trials, public hearing, commissions of inquiry and the like are settings in which the massive gap between professional

historiography and public memory might be narrowed somewhat; that is to say, in which the…public awareness of the actual history of slavery and segregation in the United States, of the extent to which it has shaped our culture and the institutions, and of the pervasive structural inequalities it has left behind could be improved.[22]

Conclusion

Weary realism, sceptical of the likelihood of immediate moral progress, is not without its attractions. To Martin Luther King's famous aphorism—'The arc of the moral universe is long but bends towards justice'—the deeply committed cynic might reply with a 'yeah, right'.

Immanuel Kant tells us in his somewhat dense prose that hope is a necessary postulate of the practical reason. He means that only by hoping can you actually do the right thing. Give up on hope, and you will give up on your responsibility to do what is good, right, just, and true. Hope is not warranted. It is just what you must hold on to.

There is no need for the advocate of reparations to be a wide-eyed innocent, thinking that justice is around the very next bend. Many things, including rather sturdy vested interests, long standing prejudices, historical ignorance, and more, stand between us and doing what is right. But even allowing for a good dose of realism in the mix, hope is not only necessary but also not wholly unrealistic. The campaigns for the abolition of the slave trade and the subsequent campaigns for the abolition of slavery itself would not have attracted cautious gamblers had bookmakers being offering odds way back then. And yet, in a relatively short stretch of the arc of the universe, justice was, in all its imperfections, partially realized.

The modern case for reparations seeks, in effect, to ensure that the compensation, which went in the wrong direction in the 1830s, is redirected properly two hundred years later. It is not unreasonable to hope that this goal will be achieved, but in the meantime, sitting on our hands is not hope's best assistant.

In Conclusion

'Everything Is What It Is...'

There is one objection to reparations that I regularly encounter, which I have saved to the end. It is all very well to advocate for reparations for the Caribbean, I am often told, but there could be many other claims against the UK, from other nations or peoples who have been harmed by our colonial or other enterprises. There is almost no stretch of the globe where Britain wasn't once busy going about its business and minding everyone else's. We couldn't settle with all the possible complainants without being bankrupted.

In a funny way, I always feel rather glad to hear this objection. The initial reaction to the idea of making reparations to the Caribbean is usually that the claim is without any merit whatsoever for the sort of reasons we have reviewed—slavery was legal at the time, Africans were involved in selling Africans, you shouldn't visit the sins of the fathers on the children, and so on and so on. So to have reached the point where the objection is now not that the claim is bad, but rather that it is one of too many good ones, is something of a step in the right direction.

What however, is the answer to this final point?

On a recent visit to the International Slavery Museum in Liverpool, the object that spoke most forcefully to me was labelled a Lady's Silver Hand Whip—it 'was owned by a lady and would have been used to punish domestic slaves. It is made of chased silver and leather.' The whip is relatively small, to suit a lady's hand, and to allow for its use in a confined space. But although its design is attentive to its purpose and so utilitarian, the object is also aestheticized—the chased silver decorates the handle and renders this an attractive luxury item. If it were on sale today it is the sort of thing you might find in one of those high-end boutiques in the halls of a shiny new airport—boutiques which most of us don't enter, knowing only too well that the single item we might just afford is the bag in which they place the goods they sell, not the goods themselves.

'Everything is what it is and not another thing' is a maxim attributed to Joseph Butler, an eighteenth-century moral philosopher. It seems to state the crashingly obvious—or it is a truism, as we more politely say. But stating the crashingly obvious is not always without a point or purpose. And the point of citing the maxim here is to encourage us to attend to the particularities of the wrong which was enslavement and its legacies, as against any general class of wrongs, of which there may be very many.

The whip was one of the symbols of the oppression of the plantation. And when in 1838 in Falmouth, Jamaica, a group of the formerly enslaved gathered to celebrate the final death of the apprenticeship system and so of slavery, they solemnly placed a whip, an iron chain and a punishment collar in the coffin inscribed 'Colonial Slavery, died July 31st, 1838, aged 276', which they buried to mark the death of the 'monster'.[1] But the whip in the museum in Liverpool tells us that one of the most telling symbols of a system of brutal violence and punishment became an everyday domestic item, and one which could be fashionably made for the delicate hands of a lady, and so as to be used not in the fields or workshops or factories of the sugar estates but in the home itself. The object is resonant because it speaks of the domestication of slavery. Slavery became ordinary and everyday, for those who lived by it, even if it was only everyday, but never ordinary, for those who lived under it. In particular the whip to be used in the home was part of a system of the use and abuse of human beings which not only removed them from home but effectively denied them any secure enjoyment of the comforts and consolations of home and family.

Wrongs come in many shapes and sizes. The Irish famine is one thing. The Bengal famine is another. In colonies in Asia and Africa, in the Americas and in the Pacific, in Australasia and across the Middle East, injuries were suffered and injustices were committed. But, to use Beckles' most resonant terms, Europeans converted the Caribbean into a 'criminal ecosystem' designed to 'accumulate wealth without cultural or ethical constraints'.[2] Human beings were kidnapped, displaced, rendered chattels to be bought and sold, forced into deathly labour regimes in violent prison camps, all of it outside norms governing other interactions between peoples and states. So if reckoning with legacies of enslavement calls for our attention first of all, it is not just because a claim has been made by CARICOM, but because of the extent of the crime, its depth, and significance for the day-by-day and hour-by-hour existence of its victims, and because of its continuing significance into the present for those who still benefit and for those who suffer as a result of the grievous wrongs committed.

There is a temptation to think about reparations as to do with the past. And in a manner of speaking they are—they are a way of facing up to the fact that, for the sake of the essentially useless luxury of sugar, Europe was prepared to commit a racial crime on an epic scale. But in fact they are also about our future.

On the title pages of her book, *Learning from the Germans: Race and the Memory of Evil*, Susan Neiman has two mottos drawn from two significant thinkers. From one of James Baldwin's essays, she takes the line that 'Not everything that is faced can be changed, but nothing can be changed until it is faced'; and from Stanley Cavell, she cites the claim 'History will not go away, except through our perfect acknowledgment of it.'

I'm not sure what our 'perfect' acknowledgment of history is meant to suggest, but the making of reparations, not only monetary, but also monetary, must be part of even our imperfect acknowledgment of a history which lives in the present and does not go away. A programme of reparations is about the past, but for the sake of the future—and the time for reparations is now.

ENDNOTES

Foreword

1. *Debates in Parliament—Session 1833*, 501.
2. C. Hall, N. Draper, K. McCelland, K. Donington, and R. Lang, *Legacies of British Slave-ownership: Colonial Slavery and the Formation of Victorian Britain* (Cambridge, 2014), 17.

Chapter 1

1. G.B. Nash, 'Foreword' (2000), to R.S. Dunn, *Sugar and Slaves: The Rise of the Planter Class in the English West Indies, 1624–1713* (Chapel Hill, N.C., 1972), xiii.
2. H. Beckles, *How Britain Underdeveloped the Caribbean: A Reparations Response to Europe's Legacy of Plunder and Poverty* (Kingston, 2021), ix.
3. https://www.theguardian.com/world/2020/dec/12/wealthy-mp-urged-to-pay-up-for-his-familys-slave-trade-past.
4. https://www.theguardian.com/politics/2006/nov/26/race.immigrationpolicy.
5. See T-N. Coates, 'The Case for Reparations', *The Atlantic*, 2014.
6. Hilary Beckles has been a leader in making the case for reparations, in such important works as *Britain's Black Debt: Reparations for Caribbean Slavery and Native Genocide* (Kingston, 2013) and *How Britain Underdeveloped the Caribbean: A Reparation Response to Europe's Legacy of Plunder and Poverty* (Kingston, 2021). He in turn credits Arthur Lewis (in 1939) and Eric Williams (in 1962) as early exponents of the basis of a claim from the UK. T-N. Coates' 'The Case for Reparations' in *The Atlantic*, June 2014, ignited the contemporary discussion in the USA. W.A. Darity Jr and A.K. Mullen's *From Here to Equality: Reparations for Black Americans in the Twenty First Century* (Chapel Hill, NC, 2020) and O.O. Táíwò's *Reconsidering Reparations* (New York, 2022), are two major recent contributions. In the UK Anthony Reddie makes a succinct argument in 'A Biblical and Theological Case for Reparations', chapter 8 of his *Working*

against the Grain: Re-imaging Black Theology in the 21st Century (London, 2008), and in a different key, R. Beckford's *Documentary as Exorcism: Resisting the Bewitchment of Colonial Christianity* (London, 2014), also addresses the issues. J. Thompson's *Should Current Generations Make Reparations for Slavery?* (Cambridge, 2018), is a short but incisive and valuable treatment of general questions around the topic.

Chapter 2

1. B.W. Higman, *A Concise History of the Caribbean*, 2nd ed. (Cambridge, 2021), 118.
2. On all this see K. Morgan, *Slavery and the British Empire: From Africa to America* (Oxford, 2007), chapter 3.
3. Dunn, *Sugar and Slaves*, 237.
4. See D. Eltis, 'The Traffic in Slaves between the British West Indian Colonies, 1807–1833', *Economic History Review* 25 (1972), 55–64; cited in A. Renton, *Blood Legacy: Reckoning with a Family's Story of Slavery* (Edinburgh, 2021).
5. Dunn, *Sugar and Slaves*, 314.
6. One of the most notorious cases is that of Thomas Thistlewood, who recorded his regular rape and abuse of enslaved women in his diary. See, D. Hall, *In Miserable Slavery: Thomas Thistlewood in Jamaica, 1750–86* (Kingston, 1989).
7. Altink, H., 'Representations of Slave Women in Discourses of Slavery and Abolition, 1780–1838', a Ph.D. thesis submitted to the University of Hull (2002), 42, citing evidence given to a Parliamentary Committee.
8. Verene Shepherd has made an outstanding contribution to Caribbean history in general, but in particular to the recognition of the particularity of women's experience of enslavement; see especially *Engendering Caribbean History: Cross Cultural Perspectives* (Kingston, 2011), ed. V. Shepherd.
9. G. Heuman, 'The British West Indies', in *The Oxford History of the British Empire, vol 3: The Nineteenth Century*, ed. A. Porter (Oxford, 1999), 473, citing B.W. Higman, *Slave Populations of the British Caribbean, 1807–1834* (Baltimore, 1984).
10. Higman, *A Concise History of the Caribbean*, 173.
11. Higman, *A Concise History of the Caribbean*, 160.
12. V. Brown, *The Reaper's Garden: Death and Power in the World of Atlantic Slavery* (Cambridge, Mass. 2008), 16, cited by M. Parker, *The Sugar Barons: Family, Corruption, Empire and War* (London, 2011), 287.

13. The phrase is from M. Craton, 'Reluctant Creoles: The Planters' World in the British West Indies', in B. Bailyn and P.D. Morgan, eds, *Strangers within the Realm: Cultural Margins of the First British Empire* (Chapel Hill, NC, 1991); cited in Morgan, *Slavery and the British Empire*, 49.

14. E. Williams, *Capitalism and Slavery* (Chapel Hill, NC, 1944).

15. Morgan, *Slavery and the British Empire*, 83. K. Rönnbäck, 'On the Economic Importance of the Slave Plantation Complex to the British Economy during the Eighteenth Century: A Value-Added Approach', *Journal of Global History* (2018), 13, 309–327.

16. O.N. Bolland, 'Systems of Domination after Slavery: The Control of Land and Labor in the British West Indies after 1835', *Comparative Studies in Society and History* 23 (1981), 591–619.

17. Heuman, 'The British West Indies', 476.

18. H. Johnson, *The Bahamas from Slavery to Servitude, 1783–1933* (Gainesville, FL, 1996), xiii.

19. H. Beckles, *A History of Barbados: From Amerindian Settlement to Caribbean Single Market*, 2nd. ed. (Cambridge, 2006), 138.

20. Higman, *A Concise History of the Caribbean*, 205.

21. Heuman, 'The British West Indies', 485.

22. G. Heuman, *The Killing Time: The Morant Bay Rebellion in Jamaica* (London, 1994), 97.

23. Quoted by Heuman, *The Killing Time*, 95.

24. P. Blanshard, *Democracy and Empire in the Caribbean* (New York, 1947), 17; cited by Beckles, *How Britain Underdeveloped the Caribbean*, 72.

25. Beckles, *A History of Barbados*, 151–153 and 208–209.

26. P.X. Scanlon, *Slave Empire: How Slavery Built Modern Britain* (London, 2020), 5.

27. Scanlon, *Slave Empire*, 371.

28. See H. Johnson, 'The British Caribbean from Demobilization to Constitutional Decolonization' in *The Oxford History of the British Empire*, vol. 4, *The Twentieth Century*, ed. J. Brown and W.R. Louis (Oxford: Oxford University Press, 1999), pp. 598–625.

29. Johnson, 'The British Caribbean from Demobilization to Constitutional Decolonization', 598.

30. Johnson, 'The British Caribbean from Demobilization to Constitutional Decolonization', 608.

31. Johnson, 'The British Caribbean from Demobilization to Constitutional Decolonization', 609.

32. Cited in Beckles, *How Britain Underdeveloped the Caribbean*, xi.

33. Johnson, 'The British Caribbean from Demobilization to Constitutional Decolonization', 608.
34. Johnson, 'The British Caribbean from Demobilization to Constitutional Decolonization', 611.
35. R.L. Bernal, 'The Great Depression, Colonial Policy, and Industrialisation in Jamaica', *Social and Economic Studies*, 37 (1988), 33–64; cited by Beckles, *How Britain Underdeveloped the Caribbean*, 92.
36. T.S. Simey's *Welfare and Planning in the West Indies* (Oxford, 1946), paints a bleak picture of the region's plight at the end of the Second World War.
37. Beckles, *How Britain Underdeveloped the Caribbean*, 187.
38. Beckles, *How Britain Underdeveloped the Caribbean*, 15.
39. Beckles, *How Britain Underdeveloped the Caribbean*, 166.
40. See in particular, G. Beckford, *Persistent Poverty: Underdevelopment in Plantation Economies of the Third World* (Oxford, 1972).
41. Higman, *A Concise History of the Caribbean*, 384–385. Táíwò in *Reconsidering Reparations*, 147, makes the links even clearer when he argues that 'climate justice and reparations are the same project: climate crisis arises from the same political history as racial injustice'.
42. See Hall et al., *Legacies of British Slave-ownership*, 1.
43. T. Wood, *British History* (London: Ladybird, 1996).

Chapter 3

1. Following M.U. Walker's important study, *Moral Repair: Reconstructing Moral Relations after Wrongdoing* (Cambridge, 2006); see also her 'Truth Telling as Reparations', in *Metaphilosophy*, 41 (2010), 525–545.
2. Walker, *Moral Repair*, 37.
3. Walker, *Moral Repair*, 37.
4. Luke, 19, 8–10.
5. J. Tillotson, sermons 116 and 117 in *The Works of the Most Reverend John Tillotson Containing Two Hundred Sermons and Discourses on Several Occasions*, in many editions.

Chapter 4

1. S. Donington, *The Bonds of Family: Slavery, Commerce and Culture in the British Atlantic World* (Manchester, 2020), 12.

2. D. Hancock, *Citizens of the World: London Merchants and the Integration of the British Atlantic Community, 1735–1785* (New York, 1995).

3. Hancock, *Citizens of the World*, 203–204.

4. Cited in Parker, *The Sugar Barons*, 153.

5. J. Wesley, *Thoughts upon Slavery* (London, 1774), 35.

6. W. Paley, *The Principles of Moral and Political Philosophy*, first published London, 1785, book 3, chapter 3.

7. A. Hochschild, *Bury the Chains: The British Struggle to Abolish Slavery* (London, 2005), 130.

8. Hochschild, *Bury the Chains*, 137.

9. Hochschild, *Bury the Chains*, 3.

10. Hochschild, *Bury the Chains*, 138.

11. A. Porter, 'Trusteeship, Anti-Slavery, and Humanitarianism', chapter 10 of *The Oxford History of the British Empire*, vol. III, ed. A. Porter, *The Nineteenth Century* (Oxford, 1999), 201.

12. C.L. Brown, *Moral Capital: Foundations of British Abolitionism* (Chapel Hill, NC, 2006), 2.

13. M. Taylor, *The Interest: How the British Establishment Resisted the Abolition of Slavery* (London, 2020), 276.

14. https://www.ucl.ac.uk/lbs/person/view/2146658151.

15. See footnote 6, chapter 1.

16. N. Draper, *The Price of Emancipation: Slave-Ownership, Compensation and British Society at the End of Slavery* (Cambridge, 2010), 76.

17. Draper, *The Price of Emancipation*, 76.

18. As Brown has it, *Moral Capital*, 97.

19. See Brown, *Moral Capital*, 98.

20. I. Whyte, *Scotland and the Abolition of Black Slavery, 1756–1838* (Edinburgh, 2006), 16–18.

21. Cited by Draper, *The Price of Emancipation*, 87.

22. Quoted in Renton, *Blood Legacy*, 133.

23. For a brief treatment, see 'Slavery in Islamic Africa, 1400–1800', R.T. Ware, in *The Cambridge World History of Slavery*, vol. 3, ed. D. Eltis and S.L. Engerman (Cambridge, 2011), 47–80.

24. See, e.g., 'Slavery in Non-Islamic West Africa, 1420–1820', G.U. Nwokeji, in *The Cambridge World History of Slavery*, vol. 3, ed. Eltis and Engerman, 81–110.

25. Nwokeji, 'Slavery in Non-Islamic West Africa, 1420–1820', 81.

26. J. Iliffe, *Africans: The History of a Continent*, 3rd. ed. (Cambridge, 2017), 135.

27. Brown, *Moral Capital*, 156.

28. See the authoritative and detailed: https://www.slavevoyages.org and *Atlas of the Transatlantic Slave Trade*, D. Eltis and D. Richardson (New Haven, 2010).

29. See Michael Anderson, 'The Social Implications of Demographic Change', in *The Cambridge Social History of Britain, 1750–1950*, volume 2, *People and Their Environment*, ed. F.M.L. Thompson (Cambridge, 1990), 1.

30. See, e.g., D. Wyatt, 'Slavery in Northern Europe (Scandinavia and Iceland) and the British Isles, 500–1420', in *The Cambridge World History of Slavery*, vol 2, ed. C. Perry, D. Eltis, S. Engerman, and D. Richardson (Cambridge, 2021), 482–507.

31. Renton, *Blood Legacy*, 4, citing E. Williams, *British Historians and the West Indies* (Trinidad, 1964), 182.

32. Parker, *The Sugar Barons*, 159–160.

33. See Draper, *The Price of Emancipation*, 25. And more generally, see, e.g., M. Craton, *Testing the Chains: Resistance to Slavery in the British West Indies* (Ithaca, NY, 1982).

34. Williams, *Capitalism and Slavery*.

35. A. Schopenhauer, *On the Basis of Morality*, 2nd. ed. of 1860, trans. E. Payne (Indianapolis, 1995), 166.

36. Taylor, *The Interest*, xvii.

37. Y. Sharett, ed., *The Reparations Controversy: The Jewish State and German Money in the Shadow of the Holocaust 1951–52* (Berlin, 2011), 179.

38. See, T. Judt, *Postwar: A History of Europe since 1945* (New York, 2005), 271.

39. S. Neiman, *Learning from the Germans: Confronting Race and the Memory of Evil* (London, 2019), 40.

40. Sharett, *The Reparations Controversy*, 162.

41. Cited in Darity and Mullen, *From Here to Equality*, 245.

42. T. McCarthy, 'Coming to Terms with Our Past, Part II: On the Morality and Politics of Reparations for Slavery', *Political Theory* 32 (2004), 758.

43. D. Hume, *A Treatise of Human Nature*, ed. D.F. and M.J. Norton (Oxford, 2000), 198.

44. K. Jaspers, *The Question of German Guilt*, trans. E.B. Ashton (New York, 1948), 26.

45. McCarthy, 'Coming to Terms with Our Past, Part II', 768. McCarthy cites A. Reed, 'The Case against Reparations', *The Progressive* 2000, and essays by Williams, McWhorter, and Steele in *Should America Pay?*, ed. R.A. Winbush (New York, 2003), as taking the anti-reparations line he summarizes.

46. This I take to be the central and very important claim of Olúfémi Táíwò's *Reconsidering Reparations*, with his argument being that present inequalities in vulnerability to climate change are the unjust legacy of the history of colonialism.
47. McCarthy 'Coming to Terms with Our Past, Part II', 768.
48. On which see, e.g., P. Gilroy *Against Race: Imagining Political Culture Beyond the Color Line* (Cambridge, Mass., 2000).
49. This is a theme which is important to the work of, e.g., James Baldwin, James Cone, Delores Williams (and other womanist theologians), and recently in H.L. Gates, *The Black Church: This Is Our Story, This Is Our Song* (New York, 2021).
50. J. Baldwin, *The Fire Next Time*, 1st published 1963 (London, 1990), 18.

Chapter 5

1. T. Craemer, 'Estimating Slavery Reparations: Present Value Comparisons of Historical Multigenerational Reparations Policies', *Social Science Quarterly*, vol. 96 (2015), 639.
2. See: https://caricomreparations.org/about-us/.
3. See: https://caricomreparations.org/caricom/caricoms-10-point-reparation-plan/.
4. Walker, *Moral Repair*, 204–205.
5. Darity and Mullen, *From Here to Equality*, 262.
6. Darity and Mullen, *From Here to Equality*, 263.
7. Ibid.
8. Ibid.
9. R. Ransom and R. Sutch, 'Who Pays for Slavery?', in R.A. America, ed., *The Wealth of Races. The Present Value of Benefits from Past Injustices* (Westport, CT., 1990); cited by Craemer, 'Estimating Slavery Reparations', 645.
10. K. Butler, *The Economics of Emancipation: Jamaica and Barbados, 1823–1843* (Chapel Hill, N.C., 1995), 18–19.
11. For detailed discussion, see Draper, *The Price of Emancipation*, especially chapters 2 and 3.
12. That is, the approx. 83% which accrued to the main Caribbean islands—the remainder going to owners in Mauritius, the Cape of Good Hope, Bermuda, and the Bahamas. See Draper, *The Price of Emancipation*, 138–139.

13. W.A. Green, *British Slave Emancipation* (Oxford, 1976), 119.
14. Taylor, *The Interest*, 275.
15. For definitions and data, see the Joseph Rowntree Foundation's *UK Poverty 2023*; https://www.jrf.org.uk/report/uk-poverty-2023.
16. Joseph Rowntree Foundation, *UK Poverty 2023*, 26.
17. T. Piketty, trans. A. Goldhammer, *Capital in the Twenty-First Century* (London, 2014), 471: '…in the second decade of the twenty-first century, inequalities of wealth that had supposedly disappeared are close to regaining or even surpassing their historical highs'.
18. https://www.ukwealth.tax.
19. https://www.wealthandpolicy.com/wp/WealthTaxFinalReport_FAQ.pdf.
20. https://www.voice-online.co.uk/wp-content/uploads/2023/07/The-Brattle-Report_compressed.pdf.

Chapter 6

1. Cited by Hochschild, *Bury the Chains*, 2.
2. Cited by Donington, *The Bonds of Family*, 2.
3. Porter, 'Trusteeship, Anti-Slavery, and Humanitarianism', 202.
4. Porter, 'Trusteeship, Anti-Slavery, and Humanitarianism', 203.
5. Thomas Rogers, 'The Long Shadow of German Colonialism', *The New York Review of Books*, 9 March, 2023.
6. Walker, *Moral Repair*, 228.
7. Darity and Mullen, *From Here to Equality*, Preface to the Second Edition, xv.
8. Ibid.
9. Darity and Mullen, *From Here to Equality*, xv.
10. Darity and Mullen, *From Here to Equality*, xvi.
11. Ibid.
12. https://www.cam.ac.uk/about-the-university/history/legacies-of-enslavement/advisory-group-on-legacies-of-enslavement-final-report.
13. *Dictionary of National Biography*, 'Robert Smith', online at: https://www.oxforddnb.com/.
14. This is a key finding in the important research of Sabine F. Cadeau first announced in 'Bonds and Bondage: Slave Trade Financial Instruments and the University of Cambridge Legacies of Enslavement Inquiry',

delivered at *Envisioning Reparations: Historical and Comparative Approaches*, Møller Institute Cambridge, Churchill College, 28–30 September, 2022.

15. C. Hall, 'Gendering Property, Racing Capital', *History Workshop Journal*, 78 (2014), 30.

16. Taylor, *The Interest*, 277.

17. https://www.churchofengland.org/sites/default/files/2023-01/church-commissioners-for-england-research-into-historic-links-to-transatlantic-chattel-slavery-report.pdf.

18. *Church Commissioners' Research into Historic Links to Transatlantic Slavery*, 7–8.

19. *Church Commissioners' Research into Historic Links to Transatlantic Slavery*, 8.

20. *Church Commissioners' Research into Historic Links to Transatlantic Slavery*, 6.

21. Darity and Mullen, preface to *From Here to Equality*, ix–x.

22. McCarthy, 'Coming to Terms with our Past: Part II', 765.

Chapter 7

1. See Taylor, *The Interest*, 293, and Parker, *The Sugar Barons*, 355.

2. Beckles, *How Britain Underdeveloped the Caribbean*, xii.

BIBLIOGRAPHY

Altink, H., 'Representations of Slave Women in Discourses of Slavery and Abolition, 1780–1838', a Ph.D. thesis submitted to the University of Hull (2002).

Anderson, M., 'The Social Implications of Demographic Change', in *The Cambridge Social History of Britain, 1750–1950*, volume 2, *People and Their Environment*, ed. F.M.L. Thompson (Cambridge, 1990), 1–70.

Baldwin, J., *The Fire Next Time*, 1st published 1963 (London, 1990).

Beckford, G., *Persistent Poverty: Underdevelopment in Plantation Economies of the Third World* (Oxford, 1972).

Beckford, R., *Documentary as Exorcism: Resisting the Bewitchment of Colonial Christianity* (London, 2014).

Beckles, H., *A History of Barbados: From Amerindian Settlement to Caribbean Single Market*, 2nd ed. (Cambridge, 2006).

Beckles, H., *Britain's Black Debt: Reparations for Caribbean Slavery and Native Genocide* (Kingston, 2013).

Beckles, H., *How Britain Underdeveloped the Caribbean: A Reparations Response to Europe's Legacy of Plunder and Poverty* (Kingston, 2021).

Bernal, R.L., 'The Great Depression, Colonial Policy, and Industrialisation in Jamaica', *Social and Economic Studies*, 37 (1988), 33–64.

Blanshard, P., *Democracy and Empire in the Caribbean* (New York, 1947).

Bolland, O.N., 'Systems of Domination after Slavery: The Control of Land and Labor in the British West Indies after 1835', *Comparative Studies in Society and History* 23 (1981), 591–619.

Brown, C.L., *Moral Capital: Foundations of British Abolitionism* (Chapel Hill, NC, 2006).

Brown, V., *The Reaper's Garden: Death and Power in the World of Atlantic Slavery* (Cambridge, MA, 2008).

Butler, K., *The Economics of Emancipation: Jamaica and Barbados, 1823–1843* (Chapel Hill, NC, 1995).

Coates, T-N., 'The Case for Reparations', *The Atlantic* (June 2014).

Craemer, T., 'Estimating Slavery Reparations: Present Value Comparisons of Historical Multigenerational Reparations Policies', *Social Science Quarterly*, 96 (2015), 639.

Craton, M., *Testing the Chains: Resistance to Slavery in the British West Indies* (Ithaca, NY, 1982).

Craton, M., 'Reluctant Creoles: The Planters' World in the British West Indies', in B. Bailyn and P.D. Morgan, eds, *Strangers within the Realm: Cultural Margins of the First British Empire* (Chapel Hill, NC, 1991).

Darity, W.A. Jr and A.K. Mullen, *From Here to Equality: Reparations for Black Americans in the Twenty First Century* (Chapel Hill, NC, 2020).

Donington, S., *The Bonds of Family: Slavery, Commerce and Culture in the British Atlantic World* (Manchester, 2020).

Draper, N., *The Price of Emancipation: Slave-Ownership, Compensation and British Society at the End of Slavery* (Cambridge, 2010).

Eltis, D., 'The Traffic in Slaves between the British West Indian Colonies, 1807–1833', *Economic History Review* 25 (1972), 55–64.

Eltis, D. and D. Richardson, *Atlas of the Transatlantic Slave Trade* (New Haven, 2010).

Gates, H.L., *The Black Church: This Is Our Story, This Is Our Song* (New York, 2021).

Gilroy, P., *Against Race: Imagining Political Culture Beyond the Color Line* (Cambridge, MA, 2000).

Green, W.A., *British Slave Emancipation* (Oxford, 1976).

Hall, C., 'Gendering Property, Racing Capital', *History Workshop Journal*, 78 (2014), 22–38.

Hall, C., N. Draper, K. McCelland, K. Donington, and R. Lang, *Legacies of British Slave-ownership: Colonial Slavery and the Formation of Victorian Britain* (Cambridge, 2014).

Hall, D., *In Miserable Slavery: Thomas Thistlewood in Jamaica, 1750–86* (Kingston, 1989).

Hancock, D., *Citizens of the World: London Merchants and the Integration of the British Atlantic Community, 1735–1785* (New York, 1995).

Heuman, G., *The Killing Time: The Morant Bay Rebellion in Jamaica* (London, 1994).

Heuman, G., 'The British West Indies', in *The Oxford History of the British Empire, vol 3: The Nineteenth Century*, ed. A. Porter (Oxford, 1999).

Higman, B.W., *Slave Populations of the British Caribbean, 1807–1834* (Baltimore, 1984).

Higman, B.W., *A Concise History of the Caribbean*, 2nd ed. (Cambridge, 2021).

Hochschild, A., *Bury the Chains: The British Struggle to Abolish Slavery* (London, 2005).

Hume, D., *A Treatise of Human Nature*, ed. D.F. and M.J. Norton (Oxford, 2000).

Jaspers, K., *The Question of German Guilt*, trans. E.B. Ashton (New York, 1948).

Johnson, H., *The Bahamas from Slavery to Servitude, 1783–1933* (Gainesville, FL, 1996).

Johnson, H., 'The British Caribbean from Demobilization to Constitutional Decolonization', in *The Oxford History of the British Empire*, vol. 4, *The Twentieth Century*, ed. J. Brown and W.R. Louis (Oxford: Oxford University Press, 1999), 598–625.

Judt, T., *Postwar: A History of Europe since 1945* (New York, 2005).

McCarthy, T., 'Coming to Terms with Our Past, Part II: On the Morality and Politics of Reparations for Slavery', *Political Theory* 32 (2004), 750–772.

Morgan, K., *Slavery and the British Empire: From Africa to America* (Oxford, 2007).

Nash, G., 'Foreword' (2000), to R.S. Dunn, *Sugar and Slaves: The Rise of the Planter Class in the English West Indies, 1624–1713* (Chapel Hill, NC, 1972).

Neiman, S., *Learning from the Germans: Confronting Race and the Memory of Evil* (London, 2019).

Nwokeji, G.U., 'Slavery in Non-Islamic West Africa, 1420–1820', in *The Cambridge World History of Slavery*, vol. 3, ed. D. Eltis and S.L. Engerman (Cambridge, 2011), 81–110.

Paley, W., *The Principles of Moral and Political Philosophy* (London, 1785).

Parker, M. *The Sugar Barons: Family, Corruption, Empire and War* (London, 2011).

Piketty, T., trans. A. Goldhammer, *Capital in the Twenty-First Century* (London, 2014).

Porter, A., 'Trusteeship, Anti-Slavery, and Humanitarianism', chapter 10 of *The Oxford History of the British Empire*, vol. III, ed. A. Porter, *The Nineteenth Century* (Oxford, 1999), 198–221.

Ransom R., and R. Sutch, 'Who Pays for Slavery?', in *The Wealth of Races. The Present Value of Benefits from Past Injustices*, ed. R.A. America (Westport, CT., 1990) (London, 2008).

Reddie, A., *Working against the Grain: Re-imaging Black Theology in the 21st Century* (London, 2008).

Renton, A., *Blood Legacy: Reckoning with a Family's Story of Slavery* (Edinburgh, 2021).

Report on Reparations for Transatlantic Chattel Slavery in the Americas and the Caribbean—The Brattle Report. Available at: https://www.voice-online.co.uk/wp-content/uploads/2023/07/The-Brattle-Report_compressed.pdf.

Rogers, T., 'The Long Shadow of German Colonialism', *The New York Review of Books* (9 March 2023).

Rönnbäck, K., 'On the Economic Importance of the Slave Plantation Complex to the British Economy during the Eighteenth Century: A Value-Added Approach', *Journal of Global History* (2018), 13, 309–327.

Scanlon, P.X., *Slave Empire: How Slavery Built Modern Britain* (London, 2020).

Schopenhauer, A., *On the Basis of Morality*, 2nd ed. of 1860, trans. E. Payne (Indianapolis, 1995).

Sharett, Y., ed., *The Reparations Controversy: The Jewish State and German Money in the Shadow of the Holocaust 1951–52* (Berlin, 2011).

Shepherd, V., ed. *Engendering Caribbean History: Cross Cultural Perspectives* (Kingston, 2011).

Simey, T.S., *Welfare and Planning in the West Indies* (Oxford, 1946).

Táíwò, O.O., *Reconsidering Reparations* (New York, 2022).

Taylor, M., *The Interest: How the British Establishment Resisted the Abolition of Slavery* (London, 2020).

Thompson, J., *Should Current Generations Make Reparations for Slavery?* (Cambridge, 2018).

Tillotson, J., *The Works of the Most Reverend John Tillotson Containing Two Hundred Sermons and Discourses on Several Occasions.*

Walker, M.U., *Moral Repair: Reconstructing Moral Relations after Wrongdoing* (Cambridge, 2006).

Walker, M.U., 'Truth Telling as Reparations', *Metaphilosophy*, 41 (2010), 525–545.

Ware, R.T., 'Slavery in Islamic Africa, 1400–1800', in *The Cambridge World History of Slavery*, vol. 3, ed. D. Eltis and S.L. Engerman (Cambridge, 2011), 47–80.

Wesley, J., *Thoughts upon Slavery* (London, 1774).

Whyte, I., *Scotland and the Abolition of Black Slavery, 1756–1838* (Edinburgh, 2006).

Williams, E., *Capitalism and Slavery* (Chapel Hill, NC, 1944).

Williams, E., *British Historians and the West Indies* (Trinidad, 1964).

Wood, T. *British History* (London: Ladybird, 1996).

Wyatt, D., 'Slavery in Northern Europe (Scandinavia and Iceland) and the British Isles, 500–1420', in *The Cambridge World History of Slavery*, vol. 2, ed. C. Perry, D. Eltis, S. Engerman, and D. Richardson (Cambridge, 2021), 482–507.

INDEX

For the benefit of digital users, indexed terms that span two pages (e.g., 52–53) may, on occasion, appear on only one of those pages.